Bond

Maths
Assessment Papers

11⁺–12⁺ years
Book 1

**J M Bond and
Andrew Baines**

Nelson Thornes

First published in 1973 as Further Fourth Assessment Papers by:
Thomas Nelson and Sons Ltd

This edition published in 2007 by:
Nelson Thornes Ltd
Delta Place
27 Bath Road
CHELTENHAM
GL53 7TH
United Kingdom

12 13 14 / 10 9 8 7 6 5 4 3 2 1

A catalogue record for this book is available from the British Library

ISBN 978 1 4085 1695 9

Illustrations by Russell Parry and Sue Swales

Page make-up by Tech Set Ltd

Printed and bound in Egypt by Sahara Printing Company

Before you get started

What is Bond?

This book is part of the Bond Assessment Papers series for maths, which provides **thorough and continuous practice of all the key maths content** from ages five to thirteen. Bond's maths resources are ideal preparation for many different kinds of tests and exams – from SATs to 11+ and other secondary school selection exams.

How does the scope of this book match real exam content?

Maths 11+ - 12+ Book 1 and Book 2 are the advanced Bond 11+ books. Each paper is **pitched a level above a typical 11+ exam**, providing a greater challenge and stretching skills further. The coverage is matched to the National Curriculum and the National Numeracy Strategy and will also **provide invaluable preparation for higher level Key Stage 2 SATs performance**. One of the key features of Bond Assessment Papers is that each one practises **a wide variety of skills and question types** so that children are always challenged to think – and don't get bored repeating the same question type again and again. We believe that variety is the key to effective learning. It helps children 'think on their feet' and cope with the unexpected.

What does the book contain?

- **24 papers** – each one contains 50 questions.
- **Tutorial links throughout** – $\boxed{\text{B } 5}$ – this icon appears in the margin next to the questions. It indicates links to the relevant section in *How to do ...11+ Maths*, our invaluable subject guide that offers explanations and practice for all core question types.
- **Scoring devices** – there are score boxes in the margins and a Progress Chart on page 68. The chart is a visual and motivating way for children to see how they are doing. It also turns the score into a percentage that can help decide what to do next.
- **Next Step Planner** – advice on what to do after finishing the papers can be found on the inside back cover.
- **Answers** – located in an easily-removed central pull-out section.

How can you use this book?

One of the great strengths of Bond Assessment Papers is their flexibility. They can be used at home, in school and by tutors to:

- set **timed formal practice** tests – allow about 30 minutes per paper in line with standard 11+ demands. Reduce the suggested time limit by five minutes to practise working at speed

- provide **bite-sized chunks** for regular practice
- **highlight strengths and weaknesses** in the core skills
- identify **individual needs**
- set **homework**
- follow **a complete 11+ preparation strategy** alongside *The Parents' Guide to the 11+* (see below).

It is best to start at the beginning and work through the papers in order. Calculators should not be used.

Remind children to check whether each answer needs a unit of measurement before they start a test. If units of measurement are not included in answers that require them, they will lose marks for those questions. To ensure that children can practise including them in their answers, units of measurement have been omitted after the answer rules for some questions.

If you are using the book as part of a careful run-in to the 11+, we suggest that you also have two other essential Bond resources close at hand:

How to do ...11+ Maths: the subject guide that explains the question types practised in this book. Use the cross-reference icons to find the relevant sections.

The Parents' Guide to the 11+: the step-by-step guide to the whole 11+ experience. It clearly explains the 11+ process, provides guidance on how to assess children, helps you to set complete action plans for practice and explains how you can use the *Maths 11+ - 12+ Book 1 and Book 2* as part of a strategic run-in to the exam.

See the inside front cover for more details of these books.

What does a score mean and how can it be improved?

It is unfortunately impossible to guarantee that a child will pass the 11+ exam if they achieve a certain score on any practice book or paper. Success on the day depends on a host of factors, including the scores of the other children sitting the test. However, we can give some guidance on what a score indicates and how to improve it.

If children colour in the Progress Chart on page 68, this will give an idea of present performance in percentage terms. The Next Step Planner inside the back cover will help you to decide what to do next to help a child progress. It is always valuable to go over wrong answers with children. If they are having trouble with any particular question type, follow the tutorial links to *How to do ...11+ Maths* for step-by-step explanations and further practice.

Don't forget the website...!

Visit www.bond11plus.co.uk for lots of advice, information and suggestions on everything to do with Bond, the 11+ and helping children to do their best.

Key words

Some special maths words are used in this book. You will find them **in bold** each time they appear in the papers. These words are explained here.

acute angle	an angle that is less than a right angle
coordinates	the two numbers, one horizontal, the other vertical, that plot a point on a grid, e.g. (4, 2)
edge	an edge is where two faces meet on a 3-D shape
factor	the factors of a number are numbers that divide into it, e.g. 1, 2, 4 and 8 are all factors of 8
icosahedron	a solid with 20 plane faces
integer	a positive or negative whole number, e.g. –6, 0, 3
kite	a four-sided shape that looks like a stretched diamond
lowest common multiple	The lowest common multiple (LCM) of two numbers is found by first finding the common multiples, then writing down the lowest, e.g. the multiples of 6 are 6, 12, 18, 24, 30, 36, 42, 48, 54, etc. The multiples of 8 are 8, 16, 24, 32, 40, 48, 56, 64, 72, etc. The common multiples of 6 and 8 are 24, 48, 72, etc. So the lowest common multiple is **24**
lowest term	the simplest you can make a fraction, e.g. $\frac{4}{10}$ reduced to the lowest term is $\frac{2}{5}$
mean	a type of average. You find the mean by adding all the scores together and dividing by the number of scores, e.g. the mean of 1, 3 and 8 is 4
median	a type of average. The middle number of a set of numbers after ordering, e.g. the median of 1, 3 and 8 is 3 e.g. the median of 7, 4, 6 and 9 is 6.5 (halfway between 6 and 7)
mixed number	a number that contains a whole number and a fraction, e.g. $5\frac{1}{2}$ is a mixed number
mode	a type of average. The most common number in a set of numbers, e.g. the mode of 2, 3, 2, 7, 2 is 2
obtuse angle	an angle that is more than 90° and not more than 180°
parallelogram	a four-sided shape that has all its opposite sides equal and parallel
polygon	a 2-D shape with straight sides
prime number	any number that can only be divided by itself and 1, e.g. 2, 3 and 7 are prime numbers
range	the difference between the largest and smallest of a set of numbers, e.g. the range of 1, 2, 5, 3, 6, 8 is 7 (8 – 1)
reflex angle	an angle that is bigger than 180° and less than 360°
rhombus	a parallelogram with four equal sides and diagonals crossing at 90°
square root	any number which, when multiplied by itself, gives you the original number, e.g. 4 is the square root of 16 (4 × 4 = 16; $\sqrt{16}$ = 4)
trapezium	a four-sided shape that has only one pair of parallel sides
vertex, vertices	the point where two or more edges or sides in a shape meet

Paper 1

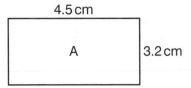
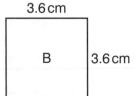

4.5 cm

A

3.2 cm

3.6 cm

B

3.6 cm

1 Area of A is _____ cm²

2 Perimeter of A is _____ cm

3 Area of B is _____ cm²

4 Perimeter of B is _____ cm

5 What is the perimeter of a square with area 81 cm²? _____ cm

Look at this number line. What numbers do the arrows point to?

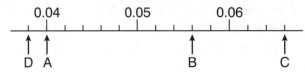

0.04   0.05   0.06

D   A   B   C

6 Arrow A points to _____

7 Arrow B points to _____

8 Arrow C points to _____

9 Arrow D points to _____

What are the missing numbers?

89	80	71
98	89	80
w	98	89

176	232	x
120	176	232
64	120	176

y	17	35
17	35	53
35	z	71

10 $w =$ _____

11 $x =$ _____

12 $y =$ _____

13 $z =$ _____

The ratio of girls to boys in a class of 25 children is 3 : 2.

14 There are _____ boys.   **15** There are _____ girls.

16–19 Here are three shaded cubes.

 A B C

B 20

Which cube has the following nets? Write either cube A, B, C or none.

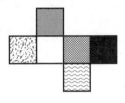 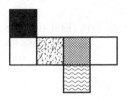 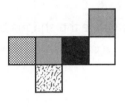

_____ _____ _____ _____

4

B 13
B 10
B 12

Class 4A has 25 children. One day 6 were absent.

20 What was the ratio of children who were present to children who were absent? _____

21 What fraction of the class was present? _____

22 What fraction was absent? _____

23 What percentage of the class was away? _____%

24 What percentage of the class was present? _____%

5

B 9

25–28 What numbers come out of the machine? Give your answers as **mixed numbers**, with fractions in their **lowest terms**.

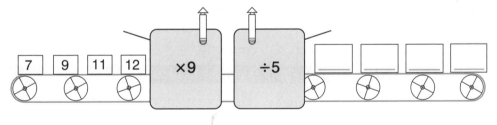

4

What number does the symbol represent in each of these equations?

B 8

29 $3 \times \Delta = 30 - 12$ $\Delta = $ _____

30 $\Delta \div 3 = 20 - 11$ $\Delta = $ _____

31 $3x = 25 + 2$ $x = $ _____

32 $2x + 1 = 36 \div 4$ $x = $ _____

4

The answers to the questions will be found in the sausage shape.

B 6

33 $13^2 =$ _____

34 $20^2 =$ _____

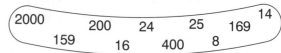

35 $2^2 + 2^2 =$ _____

36 $3^2 + 4^2 =$ _____

37–40 Complete the shapes below. The dashed line is the line of symmetry.

B 24

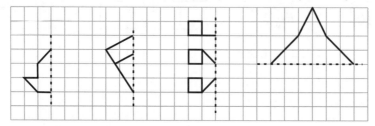

Fill each space with the sign > or < to indicate which is the larger.

41 1.7 kg _____ 1657 g

A 6

42 1.8 l _____ 1801 ml

B 25

43 days in July _____ days in June

B 27

44 $(3\frac{1}{2} + 2\frac{1}{4})$ _____ $(7\frac{1}{2} - 2\frac{1}{4})$

B 10

45 days in 2007 _____ days in 2008

B 27

46 (8×7) _____ (5×11)

B 3

47 20 hours _____ 1 day

B 27

48 4.9 cm _____ 56 mm

B 25

49   27.85
     + 36.97
     _____

50   41.10
      − 27.19
      _____

B 2

Now go to the Progress Chart to record your score!   Total   50

Paper 2

What is the order of rotational symmetry for the following shapes?

B 24

1 Rectangle   order _____

2   order _____

3 Regular pentagon   order _____

Look at this prism. How many faces, **vertices** and **edges** does it have?

4 Number of faces   _____

5 Number of **vertices**   _____

6 Number of **edges**   _____

B 21

3

Write the number of degrees contained in each of the following angles.

B 17

One right angle   Two right angles   Half a right angle

7 _____ °   **8** _____ °   **9** _____ °

$\frac{1}{6}$ of a circle   Three right angles $1\frac{1}{2}$ right angles

10 _____ °   **11** _____ °   **12** _____ °

6

13–14 Circle the two **prime numbers**.

               10   13   12   15   14   11

B 6

2

Find the cost of posting the following.

B2/B3

Airmail (Europe)	Weight up to and including	20 g	60 g	100 g	160 g	200 g	260 g	300 g	360 g
	Cost	£0.37	£0.68	£0.99	£1.44	£1.74	£2.19	£2.49	£2.94

15 2 letters, each weighing 50 g   _____

16 3 letters, each weighing 18 g   _____

17 1 letter weighing 150 g and 1 weighing 270 g   _____

18 1 letter weighing 320 g and 1 weighing 180 g   _____

19 How much change would you get from £10.00 after posting 3 letters, each weighing 310 g?   _____

20 How much change would you get from £20.00 after posting 5 letters, each weighing 280 g?   _____

6

21–24 Complete this table.

3	12	4	_____	30	14
9	144	_____	121	_____	_____

Give your answers to the following as **mixed numbers**, with fractions in their **lowest terms**.

25 $\frac{1}{2} + \frac{7}{8} =$ _____

26 $1 - \frac{7}{10} =$ _____

27 $\frac{3}{4} \times \frac{6}{9} =$ _____

28 $\frac{6}{9} \div \frac{2}{3} =$ _____

Round the following to the nearest **integer**.

29 13.46 _____

30 19.56 _____

31 99.56 _____

32 −13.36 _____

Here is a net of a model of a room, showing the walls and the floor.

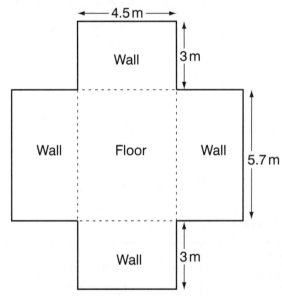

33 How high is the room? _____

34 What is the area of the floor? _____

35 What is the area of the walls? _____

36 Another room is half as long, half as wide and half as high as the room above.

What is the area of the smallest wall? _____

37 7.8 + 12.95 + 0.176 = _____

38 From 20.2 take 17.07 _____

39 Multiply 35.6 by 1.1 _____

40 Divide 72.8 by 0.4 _____

Write the **square root** of the following.

41 $\sqrt{49}$ _____   **42** $\sqrt{121}$ _____   **43** $\sqrt{81}$ _____   **44** $\sqrt{144}$ _____

Card labels for presents are sold in packs. Use the graph to answer the following questions.

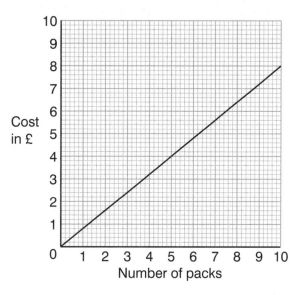

Cost in £ (vertical axis)
Number of packs (horizontal axis)

45 How many packs could I buy for £20.00?   _____

46 How much would 12 packs cost?   _____

At the supermarket there are various sizes of *Disho*.

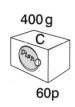
400 g
C
60p

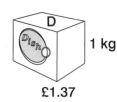
D
1 kg
£1.37

200 g
E
29p

125 g
A
19p

250 g
F
37p

750 g
B
£1.08

47 How much does 1 kg of box F cost?   _____

48 Box _____ is the best bargain.

49 Box _____ is the most expensive per kilogram.

50 How much would 1 kg of the powder in box B cost?   _____

Now go to the Progress Chart to record your score!   Total   50

Your task is to guide the robot along the white squares on the plan.

It starts and finishes on the squares marked A, B, C, D or E.

It can only move FORWARD, TURN RIGHT 90° and TURN LEFT 90°.

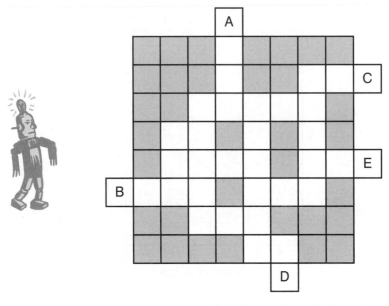

What is the next instruction needed to send the robot along the path with the least number of instructions:

1 from A to B?

FORWARD 3, TURN RIGHT 90°, FORWARD 1, TURN LEFT 90°, _____, ...

2 from B to C?

FORWARD 3, TURN LEFT 90°, _____, ...

3 from D to A?

FORWARD 1, TURN LEFT 90°, FORWARD 1, TURN RIGHT 90°, _____, ...

4 from E to B?

FORWARD 2, TURN RIGHT 90°, _____, ...

Look at this number line. What numbers do the arrows point to?

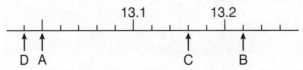

5 Arrow A points to _____

6 Arrow B points to _____

7 Arrow C points to _____

8 Arrow D points to _____

9–11 Madeleine used this decision tree to sort **integers** from 1 to 99. What is missing from the tree? Fill in the gaps.

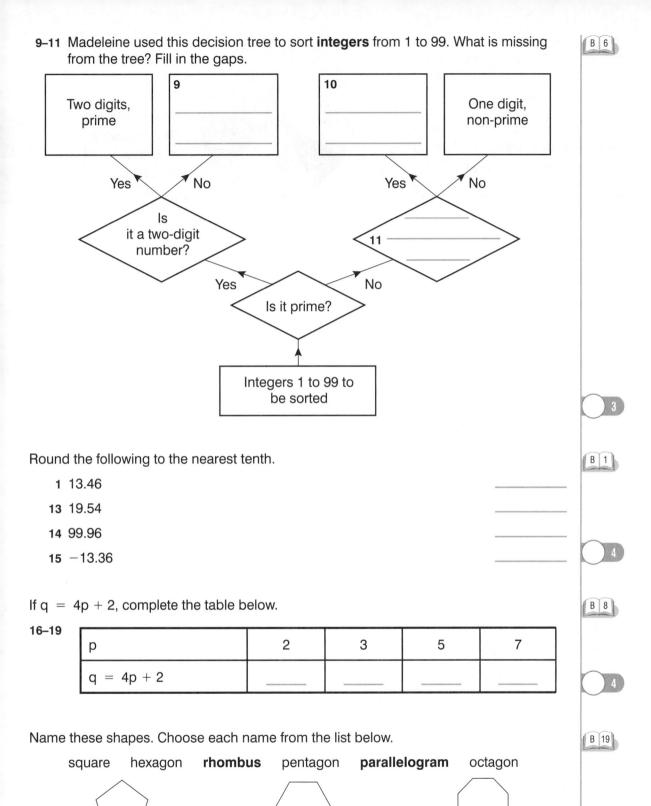

Two digits, prime

9 _____ _____

10 _____ _____

One digit, non-prime

Yes   No   Yes   No

Is it a two-digit number?

11 _____ _____ _____

Yes   No

Is it prime?

Integers 1 to 99 to be sorted

3

Round the following to the nearest tenth.

  1 13.46   _____

13 19.54   _____

14 99.96   _____

15 −13.36   _____

4

If $q = 4p + 2$, complete the table below.

16–19

p		2	3	5	7
$q = 4p + 2$		_____	_____	_____	_____

4

Name these shapes. Choose each name from the list below.

   square   hexagon   **rhombus**   pentagon   **parallelogram**   octagon

20 _____   **21** _____   **22** _____

3

Here is a pie chart which shows what Jackie did with the £48.00 she was given for Christmas. Work out the following.

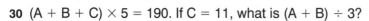

B14/B3

Savings
Scarf
Book
Magazines
Chocolates
Game
Disco

23–24 She saved _____ .

The scarf cost _____ .

25–26 The game cost _____ .

The chocolates cost _____ .

27–28 The book cost _____ .

The magazines cost _____ .

29 Jackie spent _____ at the disco.

30 $(A + B + C) \times 5 = 190$. If $C = 11$, what is $(A + B) \div 3$? _____

31 If $(L + M - N) = 68$ and $M = 31$, what is $(L - N) \div 2$? _____

Answer the following. Use **mixed numbers** where appropriate and write fractions in their **lowest terms**.

32 $2\frac{3}{5} \div 1\frac{1}{2} =$ _____   **33** $3\frac{1}{2} \div 2\frac{1}{3} =$ _____   **34** $5\frac{1}{3} \div 2\frac{1}{6} =$ _____

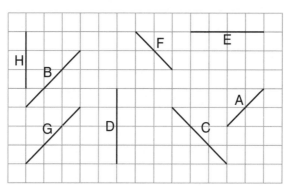

35 Line A is parallel to line G. True or False? _____

36 Line E is perpendicular to line F. True or False? _____

37 Which line is horizontal? _____

38–40 Which lines are perpendicular to F? _____

Underline the correct answer.

41 $\frac{1}{2} - \frac{1}{8} =$ $\frac{1}{6}$ $\frac{1}{10}$ $\frac{3}{8}$ $\frac{1}{2}$ $\frac{1}{4}$

42 $\frac{3}{4} \times \frac{1}{4} =$ 1 $\frac{1}{4}$ $\frac{4}{8}$ $\frac{4}{16}$ $\frac{3}{16}$

43 10% of 50 =   5   45   10   40   15

44 The number of hours in 3 days =   60   36   84   72   90

45 The number of seconds in 5 minutes =   60   300   360   120   200

46 $\frac{1}{2} \div 4 =$ 2 $\frac{1}{2}$ $\frac{1}{8}$ $\frac{3}{8}$ $\frac{3}{5}$

7

B 8

2

B 10

3

B 17

6

B10/B12

B 27

6

Work out the following.

47 $700 \div 25 = $ _____

48 $98.4 \div 24 = $ _____

49 $\begin{array}{r} 364 \\ \times \quad 25 \\ \hline \\ \hline \end{array}$

50 $\begin{array}{r} 173 \\ \times \quad 3.6 \\ \hline \\ \hline \end{array}$

4

Now go to the Progress Chart to record your score!   **Total**   50

Paper 4

Find the surface area of these cubes.

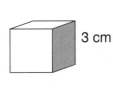 3 cm

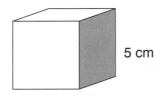 5 cm

 2 cm

1 _____ cm²

2 _____ cm²

3 _____ cm²

3

Alison waited for the Christmas sales before buying new clothes. She went to her favourite store where the prices were cut by 20%. Complete this table.

4–13

	Usual price	**Sale price**	**Saving**
Skirt	£25.00	_____	_____
Sweater	£20.00	_____	_____
Shoes	_____	£16.00	_____
Jacket	_____	_____	£5.00
Jeans	£18.00	_____	_____

14 Altogether, Alison spent _____ on her new clothes.

15 She saved _____ by waiting for the sales.

12

Fill in the missing **factors** of the following numbers.

16 The factors of 21 are   1   3   _____   21

17–19 The factors of 18 are   _____   2   _____   6   _____   18

4

20 Share 48 items in the ratio of 3 : 5. _____ : _____

21 Share 27 items in the ratio of 7 : 2. _____ : _____

22 Share 36 items in the ratio of 5 : 4. _____ : _____

23 Share 66 items in the ratio of 8 : 3. _____ : _____

24 Share 108 items in the ratio of 9 : 3. _____ : _____

B 13
5

Multiply each number below by 100.

B 1

25 47.6 _____ **26** 12 _____

27 7.2 _____ **28** 355.8 _____ **29** 0.014 _____

5

In each of the classes below there are 30 children. The table shows attendances for one week this term. Write the mean attendance for each class.

B14/B15

30–33

	Class 1A	Class 1B	Class 2A	Class 2B
Monday	27	28	30	30
Tuesday	28	23	29	25
Wednesday	30	24	28	28
Thursday	25	25	28	26
Friday	25	25	30	21
Mean attendance	_____	_____	_____	_____

34 On which day were there the most children at school? _____

35 On which day were the fewest children present? _____

36 Which class had full attendance on two days? _____

37 Which class had the lowest attendance on any one day? _____

8

Write the following numbers in figures.

B 1

38 Twenty-three thousand and seventeen _____

39 Four hundred and two thousand and forty-two _____

40 Five hundred and fifteen thousand, five hundred and five _____

41 Ninety thousand, seven hundred and nine _____

42 One hundred and one thousand and seven _____

43 Fifty-seven thousand, five hundred and seventy _____

6

Find the cost of the following.

B3/B25
B 2

44 4 kg of carrots @ 68p per kg £ _____

45 $2\frac{1}{2}$ kg of sprouts @ £1.30 per kg £ _____

46 $1\frac{1}{4}$ kg of onions @ 44p per 500 g £ _____

47 Total cost £ _____

48 How much change would you get from a £10 note? £ _____ 5

Measure these lines to the nearest millimetre.

B 26

49 ────────────────────── _____ mm

50 ────────────────── _____ mm 2

Now go to the Progress Chart to record your score! **Total** 50

Paper 5

Name the following quadrilaterals.

B 19

Choose from: square, rectangle, **rhombus**, **parallelogram** and **trapezium**.

1 _____

2 _____

3 _____  3

Simplify the following expressions.

B 8

4 a + a + a = _____   **5** a + 2a + a = _____ 2

Look at the shape below. Write the **coordinates** of each corner, starting at A.

B23/B19

6 A (_____, _____)   **7** B (_____, _____)

8 C (_____, _____)   **9** D (_____, _____)

10 E (_____, _____)   **11** F (_____, _____)

12 G (_____, _____)   **13** H (_____, _____)

14 What is the name of this shape?

_____ 9

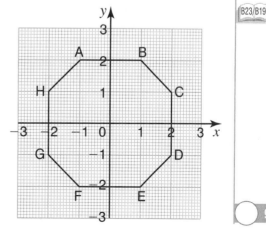

I have a normal pack of 52 playing cards.
Give your answers as fractions in their **lowest terms**.

B16/B10

15 What chance is there that I can draw out a red card? _____

16 What chance is there that I can draw out a spade? _____

17 What chance is there that I can draw out a king? _____

18 What is the chance that I can draw out a black ace? _____

19 What is the chance that I can draw out a red queen? _____

5

Find the **median** of:

B 15

20	5	15	20	10	30	The **median** is _____
21	19	12	24	18	17	The **median** is _____
22	36	8	27	22	24	The **median** is _____
23	10	80	70	60	50	The **median** is _____

4

24 The product of two numbers is 432. One number is 12, what is the other? _____

B 3

25 The sum of two numbers is 210. The larger is 179, so the smaller is _____

B 2

2

26–31 Here is the timetable of Class 4a. Each lesson is 40 minutes long and the break lasts 20 minutes. Complete the timetable.

B 27

	Begins	**Ends**
First lesson	09:10	_____
Second lesson	_____	_____
Break	_____	10:50
Third lesson	10:50	_____
Fourth lesson	_____	12:10

6

A group of children were asked what they did last Saturday morning. Some helped with the shopping, some went for a swim, others went to the club, and 8 went to the library.

B14/B2
B 10

32 How many children were asked? _____

33 How many children went shopping? _____

34 How many went swimming? _____

35 How many went to the club? _____

36 What fraction of the children went to the library? _____

5

Put these containers in order of capacity by writing 1st in the space under the largest, and so on.

| 700 cm³ | $\frac{1}{2}$ l | 0.75 l | 600 cm³ | 1 litre |

37 _____ **38** _____ **39** _____ **40** _____ **41** _____

⬤ 5

Underline the correct answers in the following.

42 451 is divisible exactly by: 3   7   11

43 20 metres is: 2000 cm   200 cm   2000 mm

44 $3\frac{3}{5}$ is between: $3\frac{1}{2}$ and $3\frac{2}{3}$ 3.25 and 3.59 $3\frac{2}{3}$ and $4\frac{3}{4}$

45 673 − 259 If I add 100 to each number the answer will be:

                    200 more   the same   200 less

B 5
B 25
B10/B11
B 2

⬤ 4

Our group, the 'Thumpers', made this flag.

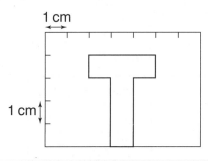

1 cm

1 cm

46 What is the area of the whole flag?   _____

47 What is the area of the 'T'?   _____

48 What is the area of the background?   _____

49 The perimeter of the flag is   _____

50 The perimeter of the 'T' is   _____

B 20

⬤ 5

Now go to the Progress Chart to record your score!   Total ⬤ 50

Paper 6

Simplify the following expressions.

1 3c + c + 2c = _____   **2** 5a − 3a + a = _____

B 8

⬤ 2

100°   100°

$x°$

3 Angle x = _____ °

$y°$ 55°

36°   40°

4 Angle y = _____ °

B 17

⬤ 2

This map shows ferry routes from the south of England to Spain and France. The table has distances of major cities from ferry ports.

Lara lives 100 miles from Plymouth and 50 miles from Portsmouth. If she takes the Plymouth to Santander ferry instead of the Plymouth to Roscoff ferry she would save 562 miles driving from her journey to Madrid.

Port of arrival — Destination	Santander	St Malo	Roscoff
Barcelona	450	719	747
Madrid	247	773	809
Alicante	508	940	976
Granada	518	1044	1080
Valencia	454	825	861
Marbella	628	1154	1190
Lisbon	553	1097	1133
Faro	626	1249	1209
Distance in miles			

5–7 How many miles will she need to drive from home for these journeys?

Ferry from	Ferry to	Destination	Driving distance
Plymouth	Santander	Alicante	_____ miles
Plymouth	Roscoff	Granada	_____ miles
Portsmouth	St Malo	Lisbon	_____ miles

8 By choosing the right ferry, the shortest possible driving distance from Lara's home to Barcelona is _____ miles.

9 Her minimum driving distance to Lisbon is _____ miles.

Look at this number line. What numbers do the arrows point to?

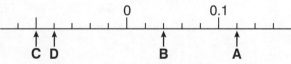

10 Arrow A points to _____

11 Arrow B points to _____

12 Arrow C points to _____

13 Arrow D points to _____

If £1 is €2, indicate which is larger by writing > or < in each space.

14 £3.54 _____ €7.00   **15** €0.91 _____ £0.45   **16** £0.34 _____ €0.70

17   4765
           8439
         + 3856
         _____

18   10000
        −   719
        _____

19   478
         × 304
         _____

20 1794 ÷ 78 = _____

21 Line H is parallel to line F. True or False?   _____

22 Line A is perpendicular to line D. True or False?   _____

23 Line E is a horizontal line. True or False?   _____

24 Which line is perpendicular to line C?   _____

25 How many lines are NOT parallel to any other lines?   _____

26 It is Sunday 28th October and the clocks have been put back during the night as Summer Time has finished. Marianne has not altered her watch, which shows 8:30 a.m. What is the correct time?   _____

27–30 Put these fractions in order of size, largest first.

$\frac{1}{12}$ $\frac{2}{3}$ $\frac{2}{5}$ $\frac{1}{8}$

_____   _____   _____   _____

31 How many glasses which hold 250 ml can I fill from a jug which holds 7.5 l?   _____

32 What is the difference between 27 m and 413 cm? Give your answer in cm.   _____

33–37 Here are four shaded cubes.

 A B C D

Which cube has the following nets? Write either cube A, B, C, D or none.

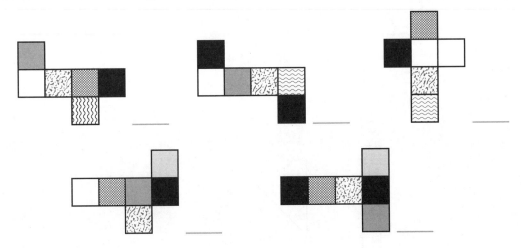

_____

_____

_____

_____

_____

Write these times as you would see them on a 24-hour clock.

38 7:05 a.m. _____

39 12:30 a.m. _____

40 10:01 a.m. _____

41 11:04 p.m. _____

Give your answers to the following calculations as **mixed numbers**, with fractions in their **lowest terms**.

42 $\frac{1}{2} + \frac{5}{8} =$ _____

43 $\frac{3}{4} + \frac{7}{16} =$ _____

44 $\frac{7}{8} + \frac{23}{24} =$ _____

45 $\frac{4}{5} + \frac{3}{10} =$ _____

46 Add together 78p, £7.99 and £3.75. _____

47 From 4 litres, take 243 cm^3. _____ cm^3

48–50 Link up the equations which give the same value of p.

3p + 5 = 12   3p = 10

3p − 4 = 13   3p = 7

3p + 2 = 12   3p = 17

Now go to the Progress Chart to record your score!   Total   50

Paper 7

1–3 Complete the table of values to satisfy the rule $y = x + 4$.

B 8

x	3	5	7	_____	20	24
$y = x + 4$	7	9	_____	13	_____	28

3

Fill in the missing number in each calculation.

B1/B3

4 $13.5 \times$ _____ $= 135$

5 $7.6 \div$ _____ $= 0.076$

6 $14.5 \div$ _____ $= 0.145$

7 $82.3 \times$ _____ $= 823$

8 $300 \div$ _____ $= 30$

9 $0.011 \times$ _____ $= 0.11$

10 $0.5678 \div$ _____ $= 0.005678$

11 $40.4 \times$ _____ $= 4040$

8

Match the percentages with the fractions. Write the correct letter in each space.

B10/B12

$\frac{1}{2}$	$\frac{3}{7}$	$\frac{7}{8}$	$\frac{1}{8}$	$\frac{3}{8}$	$\frac{1}{4}$	$\frac{5}{8}$	$\frac{3}{20}$
A	B	C	D	E	F	G	H

12 $15\% =$ _____ **13** $12.5\% =$ _____ **14** $62.5\% =$ _____ **15** $87.5\% =$ _____

4

16–20 Leila uses this decision tree to sort all the **integers** from 1 to 20. What is missing from the tree? Fill in the gaps.

B5/B6

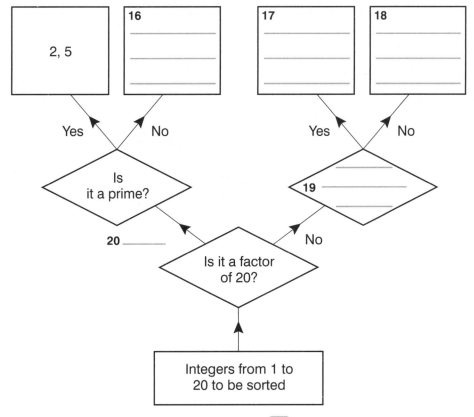

5

21–23 Underline the fractions below which are less than $\frac{1}{2}$.

$\frac{3}{7}$ $\frac{7}{10}$ $\frac{3}{4}$ $\frac{4}{9}$ $\frac{5}{6}$ $\frac{5}{11}$

B 10
3

Give the answers to the following in their **lowest terms**. Give the answers as **mixed numbers** where appropriate.

24 $\frac{5}{6} \times \frac{36}{25} =$ _____

25 $\frac{3}{11} \times \frac{55}{30} =$ _____

26 $\frac{3}{7} \times \frac{28}{21} =$ _____

27 $\frac{2}{9} \times \frac{180}{6} =$ _____

B 10
4

28 If $(X + Y + Z) \times 4 = 300$ and $X = 16$, what is $(Y + Z) \div 3$? _____

29 $3 \times (C + D - E) = 66$. If $E = 2C$ and $E = 18$, then what is D? _____

B 8
2

Remember to work out brackets first, then $\div$ and $\times$ then $+$ and $-$.

Find the answers to the following. Give answers to one decimal point where appropriate.

B2/B3
B 11

30 $5.3 + 4.7 \times 10 =$ _____

31 $4 - (5 + 7) \div 3 =$ _____

32 $14 + (24 - 4 \div 2) =$ _____

33 $(12 + 6 \times 2) - 14 \div 5 + 2 =$ _____

34 $30 + 15 \div 3 \times 2 - 14 + (5 - 8) =$ _____

5

Indicate which temperature is higher by writing $>$ or $<$ in each space.

35 $-4\,°C$ _____ $5\,°C$

36 $-3\,°C$ _____ $-2\,°C$

37 $-14\,°C$ _____ $-19\,°C$

A6/B6
3

Triangle A is rotated about the origin (0, 0).

38–41 Which of the triangles B to H
are not a rotation of A about the origin?

_____   _____

_____   _____

B 23

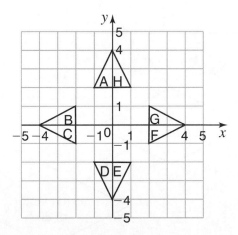

Using a protractor, measure the following angles to the nearest 10°.

B 26

42 _____   **43** _____   **44** _____   **45** _____

4

The letters from the word **ASSESSMENT** are placed in a tub and a letter is taken out at random. Writing your answers as fractions in their **lowest terms**, what is the probability of taking out a letter:

B16/B10

46 S? _____

47 E? _____

48 M? _____

49 T? _____

4

Simplify the following expression.

B 8

50 3c + 4d + 5d − c = _____

1

Now go to the Progress Chart to record your score! **Total** ◯ 50

Paper 8

B27/B2

MERSEY FERRIES
TO LIVERPOOL FROM WOODSIDE

Hours	Mon-Fri	Sat	Sun
	Minutes past the hour		
06	40	45	45
07	15 35 55	20 50	20 50
08	15 35 55	20 50	20 50
09	15 35 55	15 35 55	20 50
10	15 35 55	15 35 55	20 50
11	15 35 55	15 35 55	20 50
12	15 35 55	15 35 55	20 50
13	15 35 55	15 35 55	20 50
14	15 35 55	15 35 55	20 50
15	15 35 55	15 35 55	20 50
16	15 35 55	15 35 55	20 50
17	15 35 55	15 35 55	20 50
18	15 35 55	15 35 55	20 50
19	20 50	20 50	20 50
20	20 50	20 50	20 50
21	20	20	20

1 Write the time of the last boat each day in 12-hour-clock time. _____

2 How many boats are there between 7 p.m. and 8 p.m. on Saturday? _____

3 The boats sail every _____ minutes between 7 a.m. and 7 p.m. Monday to Friday.

4 How many more boats are there on a Wednesday than on a Sunday? _____   4

21

Your task is to guide the robot along the white squares on the plan.

It starts and finishes on the squares marked A, B, C, D or E.

It can only move FORWARD, TURN RIGHT 90° and TURN LEFT 90°.

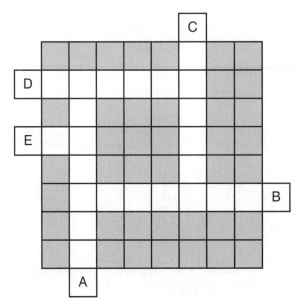

5 Which journey has the most number of instructions? _____

6 Which journey is FORWARD 2, RIGHT 90°, FORWARD 7? _____

7 Which journey is the shortest of those with only one turn? _____

8 Complete these instructions to get from C to A.

_____, TURN RIGHT 90°, FORWARD 4, TURN LEFT 90°, FORWARD 3   **4**

Find the value for x which makes these equations true.

9 $x + 6 = 13$ $x =$ _____

10 $x + 6 + 2 = 13$ $x =$ _____   **2**

A **parallelogram** has all its opposite sides equal and parallel.

A **rhombus** is a **parallelogram** with four equal sides and diagonals crossing at 90°.

A **trapezium** has only one pair of opposite parallel sides.

A **kite** has two pairs of adjacent sides of equal length and no parallel sides. Its diagonals cross at 90°.

Name each of these shapes.

11 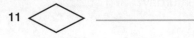 _____   12 _____

13 _____   14 _____   **4**

This pie chart shows which TV programmes are preferred by 72 children at a school.
The size of each angle in the pie chart has been given.

15 How many children like music best? _____

16 The number who like sport best is _____

17 How many children like quiz programmes best? _____

18 The number of children who like horror films best is _____

B 14

Look at this number line. What numbers do the arrows point to?

19 Arrow A points to _____

20 Arrow B points to _____

21 Arrow C points to _____

B 26

22–25 The shapes below are all regular. You are given the perimeter of each one. Work out the length of each side.

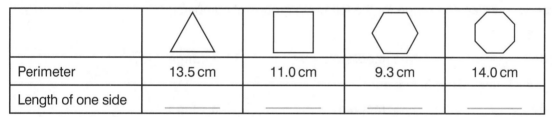

	△	▢	⬡	⬡
Perimeter	13.5 cm	11.0 cm	9.3 cm	14.0 cm
Length of one side	_____	_____	_____	_____

B 20

Write approximate answers to the following.

26 $39 \times 20 =$ _____

27 $39 + 69 =$ _____

28 $300 \div 49 =$ _____

29 $700 - 199 =$ _____

30 $63 \times 101 =$ _____

31 $6000 \div 99 =$ _____

32 $48 \times 52 =$ _____

33 $179 + 19 =$ _____

B3/B2

34–40 Complete these fractions so that they are each equivalent to 2.

$$2 = \frac{}{5} = \frac{}{11} = \frac{}{8} = \frac{}{7} = \frac{}{12} = \frac{}{27} = \frac{}{18}$$

B 10

Underline the correct number of:

41 degrees in the angles all round a point   300   90   180   360   540

42 hours in a week   140   168   24   60   186

43 metres in a kilometre   1000   100   10 000   200   10

44 millimetres in 10 centimetres   10   1000   50   5   100

B17/B27
B 25

45 days in a leap year	365	360	165	366	200
46 pence in £100	1000	10 000	100 000	100	1100
47 minutes in $\frac{3}{4}$ hour	30	60	45	15	40
48 seconds in $\frac{1}{2}$ hour	30	18 000	1800	6000	180

Measure the lines to the nearest millimetre.

B 26

49 ——————————————— _____ mm

2

50 ————————————————————— _____ mm

Now go to the Progress Chart to record your score! **Total** 50

Paper 9

Find the **mode**, **median** and **range** for the following groups of numbers.

B 15

3   5   7   3

1 mode _____   **2 median** _____   **3 range** _____

5   8   4   8   3

4 mode _____   **5 median** _____   **6 range** _____   6

7 Reflect the flag F in the y-axis (vertical axis) and label it G.

B 23

8 Reflect the flag F in the x-axis (horizontal axis) and label it H.

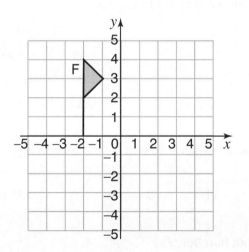

2

Find the value for x which makes these equations true.

B 19

9 $x + 6 + 2 = 13 + 2$ $x =$ _____

10 $x + 6 - 3 = 13 - 2$ $x =$ _____   2

Fill in the missing **factors** of the following numbers.

11–12 The **factors** of 35 are   1   _____   _____   35

13–15 The **factors** of 24 are   1   2   3   _____   _____   _____   12   24

16 $3\frac{3}{4} + 2\frac{7}{8}$ = _____

17 $7\frac{2}{3} + 4\frac{5}{9}$ = _____

18 $1\frac{3}{5} + 2\frac{3}{10}$ = _____

19 $8\frac{2}{7} + 3\frac{11}{14}$ = _____

20 $16.52 \div 7$ = _____

21 $0.639 \div 9$ = _____

22 $111.00 \div 4$ = _____

23 $10.34 \div 11$ = _____

| 13.61 | 7.24 |
| 0.2   5.4   6.4   6.22 |
| 13.52 | 0.18 |

24–25 Which two numbers add to give 11.8?   _____   _____

26–27 Which two numbers subtract to give 13.32?   _____   _____

28–29 Which two numbers add to give 19.83?   _____   _____

30–31 Which two numbers subtract to give 1?   _____   _____

32–33 Which two numbers add to give 6.4?   _____   _____

Find the areas of the following right-angled triangles.

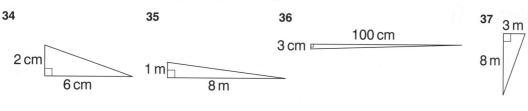

34   2 cm   6 cm

35   1 m   8 m

36   3 cm   100 cm

37   3 m   8 m

Area = ___ cm²   Area = ___ m²   Area = ___ cm²   Area = ___ m²

Write in figures the numbers shown in bold in the sentences below.

38 It was estimated that **eight and a half million** people watched the television programme.   _____

39 The population of Madrid is **two point nine million**.   _____

40 The footballer was transferred to Leeds United for **£12.2 million**.   _____

41 The building company made a profit of **£6.75 million**.   _____

Here is an approximate conversion table.
Use it to convert the measurements below.

B 25

Metric	Imperial
1 litre	$1\frac{3}{4}$ pints
1 kilogram	2.2 lb
8 kilometres	5 miles

42 4 litres ≈ _____ pints

43 10 kilograms ≈ _____ lb

44 40 kilometres ≈ _____ miles

45 _____ litres ≈ 14 pints

4

46–48 Complete the shapes below. The dashed line is the line of symmetry.

B 24

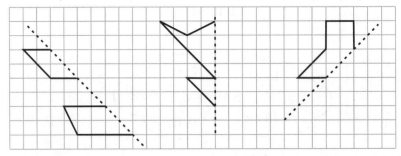

3

B 15

49 In a set of five tests Wasim got the following marks: 19   16   13   17   15.
What was his **mean** mark?

_____

50 After one more test his **mean** mark was 15. How many marks
did he score in the sixth test?

_____

2

Now go to the Progress Chart to record your score!   Total   50

Paper 10

1–3 Link up the equations which give the same value of m with a line.

B 8

5m + 3 = 8 + 7	5m = 12
5m − 2 = 32 − 14	5m = 19
5m + 6 = 4 + 21	5m = 20

3

Complete this magic square containing the numbers 2 to 10. All the rows, columns and
diagonals must add up to the same number (which is $\frac{1}{3}$ of the total number). The number
in the middle square is $\frac{1}{9}$ of the sum of all the numbers.

B2/B10

4–10

7

Give the order of rotational symmetry of these shapes.

11 _____   **12** _____   **13** _____   **14** _____

15 6^2 = _____   **16** 8^2 = _____   **17** 1^2 = _____

18 20^2 = _____   **19** 9^2 = _____   **20** 11^2 = _____

21 14^2 = _____   **22** 50^2 = _____

The shapes below are made of cubes. Write the number of cubes in each shape.

23 _____   **24** _____   **25** _____

  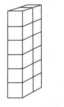

26 _____   **27** _____   **28** _____

29 $\frac{7}{8}$ of 40 = _____   **30** $\frac{5}{9}$ of 27 = _____

31 $\frac{3}{7}$ of 28 = _____   **32** $\frac{2}{11}$ of 66 = _____

Answer the following questions only using these words.

Certain   Likely   Unlikely   Impossible

33 I will eat some food today or tomorrow.   _____

34 I will eat a house today.   _____

35 It will not rain for two months.   _____

36 It will be sunny for the next twenty days.   _____

Here are some annual salaries. How much are they worth per month?

37 £25 200   **38** £21 840   **39** £13 920   **40** £17 880

_____   _____   _____   _____

B 24

4
B 6
8
B 22
6
B 10
4
B 16
4
B 3
4

A worker is paid £7.50 per hour. How many hours did he work to earn each of these amounts?

41 £150 _____

42 £262.50 _____

43 £67.50 _____

B 3
3

Here are four thermometers. What is the difference in temperature between each of the following?

44 A and B _____°C

45 B and C _____°C

46 C and D _____°C

47 A and D _____°C

B 3

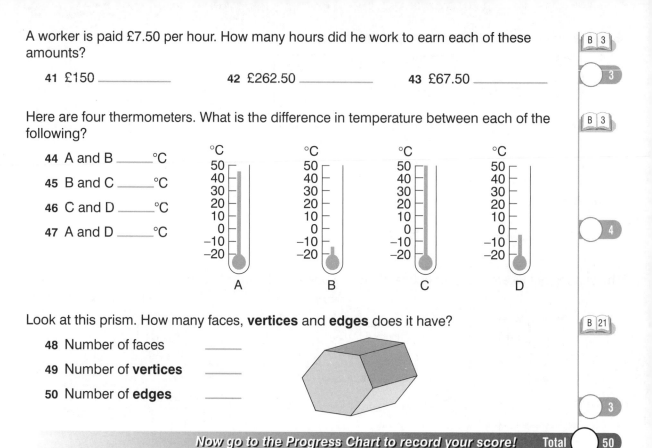

A   B   C   D

4

Look at this prism. How many faces, **vertices** and **edges** does it have?

48 Number of faces _____

49 Number of **vertices** _____

50 Number of **edges** _____

B 21
3

Now go to the Progress Chart to record your score!   Total ◯ 50

Paper 11

B2/B3

SKI PACKS		
A child is anyone under 13 years old.		
Ski boots	Adult	Child
6 Days	€40	€30
13 Days	€77	€58
Ski school 2½ hours	Adult	Child
6 Days	€142	€100
Lift passes	Adult	Child
6 Days	€164	€124
13 Days	€286	€216
Skis & sticks	Adult	Child
6 Days	€78	€46
13 Days	€154	€90

Mr and Mrs Scott took their 11-year-old daughter to France for a 6-day skiing holiday. They hired the equipment and paid for it in Euros.

1 How much did it cost for all three of them to hire ski boots? € _____

2 How much did it cost for all three of them to hire skis and sticks? € _____

3 At the time of their holiday €1.60 were equal to £1.

How much in pounds sterling did it cost to hire boots,
skis and sticks for the family? £ _____

4 In pounds sterling, the ski school cost £ _____

5 In pounds sterling, the passes for the lift cost £ _____

○ 5

B 7

What are the missing numbers?

51	36	21
66	51	36
x	66	51

52	45	y
59	52	45
66	59	52

z	290	350
290	350	410
350	410	470

6 $x =$ _____   **7** $y =$ _____   **8** $z =$ _____

○ 3

B 9

9–12 What numbers come out of the machine?

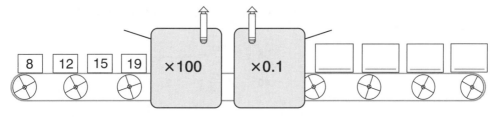

Change these fractions into percentages.

13 $\frac{16}{64} =$ _____   **14** $\frac{15}{75} =$ _____

B10/B12

○ 2

15–24 Draw lines of symmetry in the shapes below. Be careful, some shapes may have
more than one line and others may have none.

B 24

○ 10

Find the **mean** of these numbers.

B 15

25 7 $2\frac{1}{2}$ $1\frac{1}{2}$ 1   The **mean is** _____

26 4   7 $3\frac{1}{2}$ $5\frac{1}{2}$ The **mean is** _____

27 $2\frac{1}{2}$ $3\frac{1}{2}$ $4\frac{1}{2}$ $5\frac{1}{2}$ The **mean is** _____

○ 3

Find the **median** of these numbers.

28 6   9   5   7   8   The **median** is _____

29 4   10   12   11   7   The **median** is _____

30 12   6   19   13   8   The **median** is _____   ◯ 3

A class thought it would take exactly two minutes to run to the end of the field. Here are the times Mr Jones recorded.

31–36 Who was the nearest to two minutes? Put them in order in the table below.

Oliver	118 seconds
Kachanda	$2\frac{1}{4}$ minutes
Mali	107 seconds
Hermione	1 minute 59 seconds
Chloe	2 minutes 12 seconds
Jay	2 minutes 3 seconds

	Name
The nearest was	_____
Then	_____
Then	_____
Then	_____
Then	_____
Furthest away was	_____

◯ 6

Give the answers to the following in their **lowest terms**. Give answers as **mixed numbers** where appropriate.

37 $\frac{7}{12} \times \frac{132}{91} =$ _____

38 $\frac{5}{6} \times \frac{120}{70} =$ _____

39 $\frac{7}{8} \times \frac{96}{56} =$ _____

40 $\frac{9}{13} \times \frac{52}{108} =$ _____   ◯ 4

Using a protractor, measure the following angles to the nearest 5°.

41 _____   **42** _____   **43** _____   **44** _____   ◯ 4

45–48 What are the **prime numbers** less than 10? ____ ____ ____ ____   ◯ 4

Here are two irregular **polygons**. Say whether they are concave or convex.

49 _____   **50** _____   ◯ 2

Paper 12

Look at this shape.

B 17

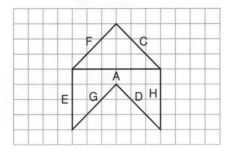

1 There are _____ pairs of parallel sides.

2 How many sides are neither parallel nor perpendicular to side G? _____

3 The difference between the number of vertical sides and horizontal sides is _____ .

3

	OCT	NOV	DEC	JAN	FEB	MAR	APR
Costa de Almeria							
Average daily hours of sunshine	7	6	6	6	6	7	8
Average daily max temp °C	20	15	10	8	9	12	15
London							
Average daily max temp °C	11	7	5	4	4	7	10

Use the table above to answer these questions.

B2/B15

4 What is the difference in average daily maximum temperature between London and Costa de Almeria in December? _____ °C

5 Write the range of average daily maximum temperatures shown for Costa de Almeria. _____ °C

6 How much difference is there between the highest and lowest average daily maximum temperatures shown for London? _____ °C

7 In which month is there the least difference in average daily maximum temperatures between the two places? _____

8 What is the difference in temperature in that month? _____ °C

5

What is the sale price of each of these items, and what is your saving on each purchase?

B12/B2

9 Sale price £ _____

10 Saving £ _____

£150

11 Sale price £ _____

12 Saving £ _____

£850

10% off

7½% off

£6

20% off

13 Sale price £ _____

14 Saving £ _____

15 What is the original price of the camera if you save £22? £ _____

16 The temperature increases by 16 °C from 10 °C. What is the new temperature? _____ °C

17 The temperature decreases by 16 °C from 10 °C. What is the new temperature? _____ °C

18 The temperature increases by 13 °C from −14 °C. What is the new temperature? _____ °C

19 The temperature decreases by 16 °C from −12 °C. What is the new temperature? _____ °C

Below are some nets of solid shapes and a list that will help you name them.

hexagonal prism   cube   octahedron   **icosahedron**

20 _____   **21** _____   **22** _____   **23** _____

Here are the hand-spans in cm for Class 6B.

| 17 | 18 | 14 | 13 | 14 | 18 | 19 |
| 17 | 21 | 23 | 16 | 11 | 13 | 10 |

24–28 Complete this frequency table.

Hand-span (cm)	0–5	6–10	11–15	16–20	21–25
No. of pupils	_____	_____	_____	_____	_____

7

B 6

4

B 25

4

B 14

5

Any answer that requires units of measurement should be marked wrong if the correct units have not been included.

Paper 1

1. 14.4
2. 15.4
3. 12.96
4. 14.4
5. 36
6. 0.04
7. 0.056
8. 0.066
9. 0.038
10. 107
11. 288
12. −1
13. 53
14. 10
15. 15
16. C
17. None
18. A
19. B
20. 19 : 6
21. $\frac{19}{25}$
22. $\frac{6}{25}$
23. 24
24. 76
25. $12\frac{3}{5}$
26. $16\frac{1}{5}$
27. $19\frac{4}{5}$
28. $21\frac{3}{5}$
29. 6
30. 27
31. 9
32. 4
33. 169
34. 400
35. 8
36. 25
37.
38.
39.
40.

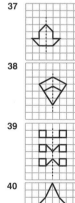

41. >
42. <
43. >
44. >
45. <
46. >
47. <
48. <
49. 64.82
50. 13.91

Paper 2

1. 2 (or 4 if square is mentioned)
2. 2
3. 5
4. 7
5. 10
6. 15
7. 90
8. 180
9. 45
10. 60
11. 270
12. 135
13–14. 10 ⑬ 12 15 14 ⑪
15. £1.36
16. £1.11
17. £3.93
18. £4.68
19. £1.18
20. £7.55

21–24.

3	12	4	**11**	30	14
9	144	**16**	121	**900**	196

25. $1\frac{3}{8}$
26. $\frac{3}{10}$
27. $\frac{1}{2}$
28. 1
29. 13
30. 20
31. 100
32. −13
33. 3 m
34. 25.65 m²
35. 61.2 m²
36. 3.375 m²
37. 20.926
38. 3.13
39. 39.16
40. 182
41. 7
42. 11
43. 9
44. 12
45. 25
46. £9.60
47. £1.48
48. D
49. A
50. £1.44

Paper 3

1. FORWARD 3
2. FORWARD 3
3. FORWARD 5
4. FORWARD 2
5. 13 or 13.0
6. 13.22
7. 13.16
8. 12.98
9. One digit, prime
10. Two digits, non-prime
11. Is it a two-digit number?
12. 13.5
13. 19.5
14. 100 or 100.0
15. −13.4
16. 10
17. 14
18. 22
19. 30
20. pentagon
21. hexagon
22. octagon
23. £12.00 or £12
24. £6.00 or £6
25. £8.00 or £8
26. £4.00 or £4
27. £6.00 or £6
28. £4.00 or £4
29. £8.00 or £8
30. 9
31. 18.5 or $18\frac{1}{2}$
32. $1\frac{11}{15}$
33. $1\frac{1}{2}$
34. $2\frac{6}{13}$
35. True
36. False
37. E
38–40. any order: A, B, G
41. $\frac{3}{8}$
42. $\frac{3}{16}$
43. 5
44. 72
45. 300
46. $\frac{1}{8}$
47. 28
48. 4.1
49. 9100
50. 622.8

Paper 4

1. 54
2. 150

Bond Maths Assessment Papers 11⁺ – 12⁺ years Book 1

ANSWERS

3 24

4–13

	Usual price	Sale price	Saving
Skirt	£25.00	**£20.00**	**£5.00**
Sweater	£20.00	**£16.00**	**£4.00**
Shoes	**£20.00**	£16.00	**£4.00**
Jacket	**£25.00**	**£20.00**	£5.00
Jeans	£18.00	**£14.40**	**£3.60**

14 £86.40
15 £21.60
16 7
17 1
18 3
19 9
20 18 : 30
21 21 : 6
22 20 : 16
23 48 : 18
24 81 : 27
25 4760
26 1200
27 720
28 35 580
29 1.4
30 27
31 25
32 29
33 26
34 Monday
35 Friday
36 2A
37 2B
38 23 017
39 402 042
40 515 505
41 90 709
42 101 007
43 57 570
44 2.72
45 3.25
46 1.10
47 7.07
48 2.93
49 84
50 51

Paper 5

1 parallelogram
2 rhombus
3 trapezium
4 3a
5 4a
6 (−1, 2)
7 (1, 2)
8 (2, 1)
9 (2, −1)
10 (1, −2)
11 (−1, −2)
12 (−2, −1)
13 (−2, 1)
14 octagon
15 $\frac{1}{2}$
16 $\frac{1}{4}$
17 $\frac{1}{13}$
18 $\frac{1}{26}$
19 $\frac{1}{26}$
20 15
21 18
22 24
23 60
24 36
25 31

26–31

	Begins	Ends
First lesson	09:10	**09:50**
Second lesson	**09:50**	**10:30**
Break	**10:30**	10:50
Third lesson	10:50	**11:30**
Fourth lesson	**11:30**	12:10

32 64
33 32
34 16
35 8
36 $\frac{1}{8}$ or $\frac{8}{64}$
37 3rd
38 5th
39 2nd
40 4th
41 1st
42 11
43 2000 cm
44 $3\frac{1}{2}$ and $3\frac{2}{3}$
45 the same
46 35 cm^2
47 6 cm^2
48 29 cm^2
49 24 cm
50 14 cm

Paper 6

1 6c
2 3a
3 160
4 49
5 608
6 1180
7 1147
8 550
9 653
10 0.12
11 0.04
12 −0.1
13 −0.08
14 >
15 >
16 <
17 17 060
18 9281
19 145 312
20 23
21 False
22 False
23 True
24 H
25 2
26 7:30 a.m.
27 $\frac{2}{3}$
28 $\frac{2}{5}$
29 $\frac{1}{8}$
30 $\frac{1}{12}$
31 30
32 2287 cm
33 B
34 D
35 None
36 C
37 A
38 07:05
39 00:30
40 10:01
41 23:04
42 $1\frac{1}{8}$
43 $1\frac{3}{16}$
44 $1\frac{5}{6}$
45 $1\frac{1}{10}$
46 £12.52
47 3757
48–50
$3p + 5 = 12$ $3p = 10$
$3p − 4 = 13$ $3p = 7$
$3p + 2 = 12$ $3p = 17$

Paper 7

1–3

x	3	5	7	**9**	20	24
$y = x + 4$	7	9	**11**	13	**24**	28

4 10
5 100
6 100
7 10
8 10
9 10
10 100
11 100
12 H
13 D
14 G
15 C
16 1, 4, 10, 20
17 3, 7, 11, 13, 17, 19
18 6, 8, 9, 12, 14, 15, 16, 18
19 Is it a prime?
20 Yes
21–23 $\frac{3}{7}$ $\frac{7}{10}$ $\frac{3}{4}$ $\frac{4}{9}$ $\frac{5}{6}$ $\frac{5}{11}$

Bond Maths Assessment Papers 11+ - 12+ years Book 1

24	$1\frac{1}{5}$

25 $\frac{1}{2}$

26 $\frac{4}{7}$

27 $6\frac{2}{3}$

28 $\frac{59}{3}$ or $19\frac{2}{3}$

29 31

30 52.3

31 0

32 36

33 23.2

34 23

35 $<$

36 $<$

37 $>$

38–41 *any order:* B, D, F, H

42 40°

43 30°

44 110°

45 120°

46 $\frac{2}{5}$

47 $\frac{1}{5}$

48 $\frac{1}{10}$

49 $\frac{1}{10}$

50 $2c + 9d$

Paper 8

1 9:20 p.m.

2 2

3 20

4 12

5 E to C or C to E

6 D to A

7 A to E or E to A

8 FORWARD 6

9 7

10 5

11 rhombus

12 kite

13 parallelogram

14 trapezium

15 18

16 6

17 12

18 9

19 0.04

20 −0.08

21 −0.22

22–25

△	□	⬡	⯃
13.5 cm	11.0 cm	9.3 cm	14.0 cm
4.5 cm	**2.75 cm**	**1.55 cm**	**1.75 cm**

26 800

27 110

28 6

---

29 500

30 6300

31 60

32 2500

33 200

34 10

35 22

36 16

37 14

38 24

39 54

40 36

41 360

42 168

43 1000

44 100

45 366

46 10 000

47 45

48 1800

49 70

50 87

Paper 9

1 3

2 4

3 4

4 8

5 5

6 5

7–8

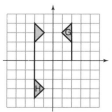

9 7

10 8

11–12 *any order:* 5, 7

13–15 *any order:* 4, 6, 8

16 $6\frac{5}{8}$

17 $12\frac{2}{9}$

18 $3\frac{9}{10}$

19 $12\frac{1}{14}$

20 2.36

21 0.071

22 27.75

23 0.94

24–25 *any order:* 5.4, 6.4

26 13.52

27 0.2

28–29 *any order:* 13.61, 6.22

30 6.4

31 5.4

32–33 *any order:* 0.18, 6.22

34 6

35 4

---

36 150

37 12

38 8 500 000

39 2 900 000

40 12 200 000

41 6 750 000

42 7

43 22

44 25

45 8

46

47

48

49 16

50 10

Paper 10

1–3

$5m + 3 = 8 + 7$ ——— $5m = 12$

$5m − 2 = 32 − 14$ $5m = 19$

$5m + 6 = 4 + 21$ $5m = 20$

4–10

7	2	9
8	6	4
3	10	5

11 1

12 5

13 4

14 2

15 36

16 64

17 1

18 400

19 81

20 121

21 196

22 2500

23 8

24 18

25 16

26 16

27 20

28 12

29 35

30 15

31 12

32 12

33 Certain

34 Impossible

35 Unlikely

36 Unlikely

Bond Maths Assessment Papers 11⁺ – 12⁺ years Book 1

37 £2100
38 £1820
39 £1160
40 £1490
41 20 hours
42 35 hours
43 9 hours
44 60
45 65
46 55
47 50
48 8
49 12
50 18

Paper 11

1 110
2 202
3 195
4 240
5 282.50
6 81
7 38
8 230
9 80
10 120
11 150
12 190
13 25%
14 20%

15–24

25 3
26 5
27 4
28 7
29 10
30 12

31–36

	Name:
The nearest was	Hermione
Then	Oliver
Then	Jay
Then	Chloe
Then	Mali
Furthest away was	Kachanda

37 $\frac{11}{13}$
38 $1\frac{3}{7}$
39 $1\frac{1}{2}$
40 $\frac{1}{3}$
41 45°
42 125°
43 225°
44 115°
45 2
46 3

47 5
48 7
49 concave
50 convex

Paper 12

1 3
2 3
3 1
4 5
5 12
6 7
7 January
8 4
9 127.50
10 22.50
11 765
12 85
13 5.55
14 0.45
15 110
16 26
17 −6
18 −1
19 −28
20 octahedron
21 icosahedron
22 hexagonal prism
23 cube

24–28

Hand-span (cm)	0–5	6–10	1–15	16–20	21–25
No of pupils	0	1	5	6	2

29–32

Key	0–5 cm	
2 children = ☺	6–10 cm	☾
	11–15 cm	☺ ☺ ☾
	16–20 cm	☺ ☺ ☺
	21–25 cm	☺

33 27
34 £18.63
35 35
36 £24.15
37 28
38 £19.32
39 £62.10
40 180
41 150
42 90
43 120
44 363
45 297
46 112 832
47 108 727 122
48 11.8
49 10.9
50 7.4

Paper 13

1 14
2 24
3 36

4–8

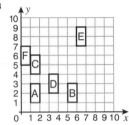

9 5, 15
10 1, 3, 7, 9, 11, 13, 17, 19
11 2, 4, 6, 8, 12, 14, 16, 18
12 Is it a multiple of 5?
13 FORWARD 4
14 TURN RIGHT 90°
15 FORWARD 1
16 TURN LEFT 90°
17 66
18 90
19 48
20 800
21 900
22 1200
23 30
24 120 or 121
25 800
26 0.773
27 5
28 20
29 18
30 8

31–33

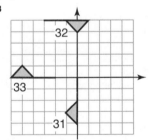

34 F
35 A
36 E
37 B
38 D
39 C
40 13 : 39 or 1 : 3
41 4 : 48 or 1 : 12
42 $\frac{1}{6}$
43 $\frac{1}{2}$
44 0
45 $\frac{2}{3}$
46 1

I think of a number then add 2	$\frac{n}{2}$
I think of a number then subtract 3	$n + 2$
I think of a number then multiply it by 4	$n - 3$
I think of a number then halve it	$4n$

Paper 14

1. 8 m
2. 15 cm
3. 15
4. 42.5
5. 55
6. 62.5
7. 9
8. 105 cm
9. 3.5 cm
10. $3\frac{8}{9}$
11. $1\frac{7}{10}$
12. $1\frac{9}{16}$
13. $2\frac{7}{9}$
14. 11
15. 2
16. 6
17. 70
18. -32
19. 13
20. 29
21. 0
22–25. *any order:* 15, 30, 35, 120
26–30. *any order:* 14, 21, 28, 35, 42

31–35

Multiply by 3 then add 2	$\frac{n}{3} - 2$
Multiply by 2 then add 3	$3n + 2$
Divide by 2 then subtract 3	$3(n + 2)$
Divide by 3 then subtract 2	$2n + 3$
Add 2 then multiply by 3	$\frac{n}{2} - 3$

36. $\frac{1}{11}$
37. $\frac{1}{11}$
38. $\frac{2}{11}$
39. $\frac{2}{11}$
40. acute
41. acute
42. reflex
43. obtuse
44. acute

45–50

At first:	Angus had **99p** or **£0.99**	Belinda had **40p** or **£0.40**	Christine had **29p** or **£0.29**
Afterwards:	Angus had **96p** or **£0.96**	Belinda had **48p** or **£0.48**	Christine had **24p** or **£0.24**

Paper 15

1. 23
2. 29
3. A
4. C
5. B and C
6. None

7–13

Perimeter	Length	Width	Area
24 cm	5 cm	7 cm	35 cm²
24 cm	**9 cm**	3 cm	27 cm²
24 cm	1 cm	**11 cm**	**11 cm²**
24 cm	**2 cm**	10 cm	**20 cm²**
24 cm	**6 cm**	6 cm	36 cm²

14. FORWARD 4
15. FORWARD 5
16. FORWARD 2
17. FORWARD 5
18. 50 miles
19. Chicago, Detroit
20. Montreal, Los Angeles
21. Denver, Jacksonville
22. Detroit, Jacksonville

23–26

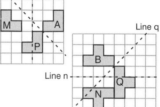

27. 92
28. -14
29. 5
30. 3
31. £3.00
32. £1.20
33. £2.40
34. £2.00
35. 4750 cm
36. 17.6 cm
37. 607 cm
38. 10 303 cm
39. 370 m
40. 11 000 m
41. 2 m
42. 4150 m

43–48

Fraction	Decimal	Percentage
$\frac{9}{10}$	0.9	90%
$\frac{1}{100}$	0.01	1%
$\frac{17}{100}$	0.17	17%

49. 4
50. 4

Paper 16

1. -9
2. -22
3-4. concave heptagon or septagon
5-6. convex octagon
7. 29
8. 2
9. 39
10. 142 minutes or 2 hours 22 minutes
11. 74.3
12. 45.7
13. 39.59
14. $\frac{1}{6}$
15. $\frac{1}{2}$
16. 0
17. $\frac{5}{6}$
18. 1
19. $<$
20. $>$
21. $>$
22. $<$

23–25

Class	Cost for the class
2a	£120
2b	£140
3a	£160

26. 9
27. 4a
28. 40

29–34

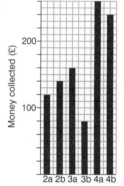

35. $\frac{5}{18}$
36. $7a + 3$
37. $5b + 4$
38. $3c + 6$
39. $3a + 5$
40. 43
41. 110
42. 33
43. 21
44. 40 cm
45. 10 cm
46. 14 cm
47. 17 cm
48. 4
49. 1
50. 6

Bond Maths Assessment Papers 11+ - 12+ years Book 1

ANSWERS

Paper 17

1 17
2 19
3 23

4–9

Time (mins)	21–25	26–30	31–35	36–40	41–45	46 and over
No of pupils	4	4	4	4	5	1

10–12

Time (mins)	0–20	21–60	61–80
No of pupils	0	22	0

13 A
14 160 cm²
15 80 cm²
16 80 cm²
17–19 *any order:* A, C, G
20 365
21 10
22 3.03 km
23 5.15 m
24 10
25 (1, 2)
26 (3, 2)
27 (2, 0)
28 (0, 0)
29 (−2, −3)
30 (−3, −1)
31 (−1, −1)
32 (2, −1)
33 (2, −3)
34 (0, −2)
35 (0, 0)
36 1
37–38 *any order:* 7.2, 7.3
39 7.3
40 7.03
41–42 *any order:* 7.23, 7.32
43 7.32
44 7.01
45–46 *any order:* 7.01, 7.2
47 12
48 12
49 10
50 18

Paper 18

1 25
2 55
3 130

4 $\frac{1}{7}$
5 $\frac{3}{7}$
6 $\frac{2}{7}$
7 0
8 >
9 >
10 <
11 <
12 <
13 >
14 600 cm²
15 160 cm²
16 440 cm²
17 300 cm²
18 50 cm²
19 250 cm²
20 40 cm³
21 24 cm³
22 14 cm³
23 27 cm³
24 320 cm³
25 192 cm³
26 112 cm³
27 216 cm³

28–33

3	2	7	**10**	8	**12**	21	24
27	18	**63**	90	**72**	108	**189**	216

34 140
35 40 608
36 12
37 9
38 24
39 3
40 42p
41 56p
42 35p
43 49p
44 42p
45 21
46 irregular
47–48 regular octagon
49–50 irregular pentagon

Paper 19

1 4
2 −9

3–11

mode	median	range
$10\frac{1}{2}$	$10\frac{1}{2}$	21
221	56	223
−3	−3	98

12 15
13 30
14 42

15 12
16 15
17 35

18–24

Shoe size	Frequency
1	1
$1\frac{1}{2}$	3
2	2
$2\frac{1}{2}$	5
3	4
$3\frac{1}{2}$	2
4	3

25–31

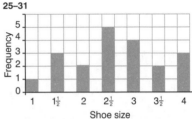

32–34

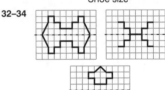

35 $\frac{1}{6}$
36 25
37 7
38 £5.25
39 £12.25
40 £5.60
41 £8.25
42 £9.45
43 £10.30
44 28
45 144
46 224
47 6
48 8
49 12
50 2

Paper 20

1 3114
2 75 501
3 3 415 833
4 24
5 £16.80
6 35
7 £24.50

8 27
9 £18.90
10 18
11 £12.60
12 $\frac{1}{2}$
13 $\frac{1}{3}$
14 $\frac{1}{6}$
15 $\frac{1}{12}$
16 $11a + 2$
17 $13b + 17$
18 $2c + 3$
19 $26p + 17$
20 25
21 $2\frac{1}{2}$ and 3
22 4
23 1.001
24 45
25 150
26 9
27 720
28 2000
29 1000
30 $\frac{1}{4}$
31 $\frac{3}{8}$
32 $\frac{1}{8}$
33 $\frac{1}{3}$
34 120 m^2
35 190 m^2
36 160 m^2
37 150 m^2
38 20%
39 80%
40 36%
41 25%
42 30%
43 50%
44 44%
45 75%
46 36
47 49
48 21
49 28
50 18 hours

Paper 21

1 118
2 5
3 $1\frac{1}{4}$ or 1.25
4 6
5 33
6 -5
7 -2
8–9 regular, hexagon
10–11 irregular, octagon
12–13 irregular, quadrilateral

---

14 18
15 2400
16–20

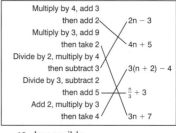

21 48
22 84
23 63
24 64
25 60
26 112
27 72
28 80
29 1439
30 -4.1
31 -3.1
32 -2.1
33 0.1
34 2.1
35 40
36 72
37 60
38 32
39 35
40 8
41 $6\frac{1}{2}$ or 6.5
42 202
43 9
44 77
45–46 any order: 72, 76
47–49 any order: 72, 75, 78
50 72

Paper 22

1 1
2 3
3 2
4 $\frac{5}{7}$
5 $\frac{1}{2}$
6 $\frac{3}{5}$
7 $\frac{4}{7}$
8 10
9 4.6
10 21
11 9
12 17
13 165
14 250
15 2250

16–31

2	×	3	+	4	=	10
+		×		×		−
4	+	1	−	2	=	3
+		−		−		−
2	×	4	−	3	=	5
=		=		=		=
8	+	−1	−	5	=	2

Column 5 also correct as:
$4 \div 2 + 3 = 5$ or
$4 - 2 + 3 = 5$
32–36 *any order:* 29, 31, 37, 41, 43
37–41

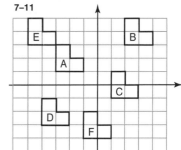

42 Impossible
43 Unlikely (or likely)
44 Unlikely
45 Likely
46 True
47 False
48 True
49 False
50 True

Paper 23

1 -11
2 0
3 -28
4 6600
5 14 400
6 5700
7–11

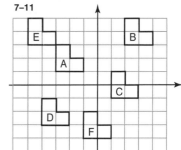

12 256.781
13 256.781
14 812.567
15 789.256
16 125.678
17 256.781
18 Any 70 to 75

19 2200
20 45
21 Any 40 to 45
22 9 or 10
23 39
24 <
25 <
26 >
27 <
28–36

Mode	Median	Range
none	100	9955
-7	-7	7
$\frac{1}{2}$	$\frac{1}{2}$	$\frac{1}{4}$

37 $67\frac{1}{2}$ or 67 years 6 months
38 11 years 3 months
39 10 years 8 months
40–41 *any order:* 1, 3
42–45 *any order:* 1, 2, 4, 8
46–50

x	-2	-1	0	1	2	3
$y = 2x + 8$	4	6	8	10	12	14

Paper 24

1 6
2 30
3 150

4 7.5
5 327 635
6 687 040
7 359 310
8 490 200
9–12 *any four from the following or equivalent*

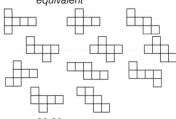

13 39.90
14 13.30
15 $\frac{6}{7}$
16 $\frac{1}{2}$
17 $1\frac{1}{2}$
18 2
19 5
20 7
21 6
22 10
23 2
24 4
25 9
26 55
27 33
28 176

29 215
30 236
31 559
32 15
33 57 532
34 341 588
35 3 415 820
36 >
37 <
38–40

Line d
Line f   Line e

41–48

Length	Width	Area
10 cm	8 cm	80 cm²
15 cm	3 cm	**45 cm²**
1 cm	**17 cm**	**17 cm²**
15.5 cm	2.5 cm	**38.75 cm²**
9 cm	**9 cm**	81 cm²

49 130
50 50

29–32 Now complete the pictogram below for these values (including the key). The last row has been done for you.

Key	0–5 cm	
____ children = ☺	6–10 cm	
	11–15 cm	
	16–20 cm	
	21–25 cm	☺

Here are the petrol gauges in three cars.

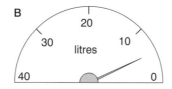
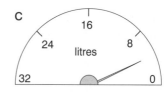

Petrol costs 69p per litre. In order to fill up their tanks:

33–34 A would need _____ litres.   This would cost _____ .

35–36 B would need _____ litres.   This would cost _____ .

37–38 C would need _____ litres.   This would cost _____ .

39 How much would it cost to fill all three cars?   _____

Give the size of the marked angles below.

40 _____ °   **41** _____ °   **42** _____ °   **43** _____ °

There are 660 pupils in a school; 55% of them are girls.

44 How many girls are in the school?   _____

45 How many boys are there?   _____

46–47 When you multiply 1243 by 4318 the last digit will end in a **4**, since 3 × 8 is **24**. Now use this information to circle the correct answer to each of the following questions.

344 × 328 =   112 835   112 832   112 831   112 839   112 838

2347 × 46 326 = 108 727 124   108 727 121   108 727 126   108 727 122   108 727 129

Write the following figures rounded correctly to one decimal place.

48 11.76 ——————   **49** 10.91 ——————

50 7.35 ——————

Now go to the Progress Chart to record your score!   **Total**   50

Paper 13

Look at this prism. How many faces, **vertices** and **edges** does it have?

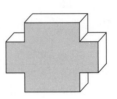

1 Number of faces   ——————

2 Number of **vertices**   ——————

3 Number of **edges**   ——————

P is a translation of A by **p**.

Translate shape A as shown below. Draw and label each new location.

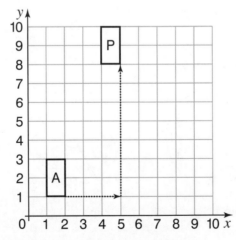

$$\mathbf{p} = \begin{pmatrix} 3 \\ 7 \end{pmatrix}$$

$$\mathbf{b} = \begin{pmatrix} 4 \\ 0 \end{pmatrix} \quad \mathbf{c} = \begin{pmatrix} 0 \\ 3 \end{pmatrix} \quad \mathbf{d} = \begin{pmatrix} 2 \\ 1 \end{pmatrix} \quad \mathbf{e} = \begin{pmatrix} 5 \\ 6 \end{pmatrix} \quad \mathbf{f} = \begin{pmatrix} -1 \\ 4 \end{pmatrix}$$

4 Translate A by **b** to B.   **5** Translate A by **c** to C.   **6** Translate A by **d** to D.

7 Translate A by **e** to E.   **8** Translate A by **f** to F.

9–12 John used this decision tree to sort **integers** from 1 to 20. What is missing from the tree? Fill in the gaps.

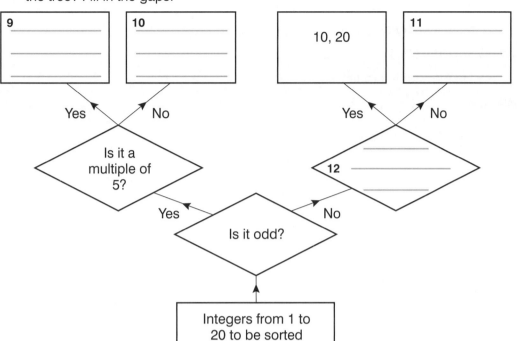

Your task is to guide the robot along the white squares on the plan.

It starts and finishes on the squares marked A, B, C, D or E.

It can only move FORWARD, TURN RIGHT 90° and TURN LEFT 90°.

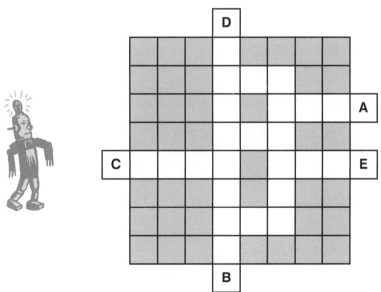

What is the next instruction to get:

13 from A to B via the shortest route?

FORWARD 3, TURN LEFT 90°, _____ , ...

14 from E to D via the shortest route?

FORWARD 3, _____ , …

15 from A to C via the shortest route?

FORWARD 3, TURN LEFT 90°, _____ , …

16 from C to E via the shortest route?

FORWARD 4, _____ , …

Find the surface area of these cuboids.

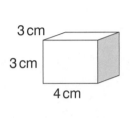

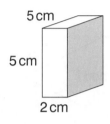

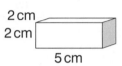

17 _____ cm²

18 _____ cm²

19 _____ cm²

Estimate the answers to the following calculations.

20 598 + 204 =

21 1212 − 297 =

22 39 × 31 =

23 902 ÷ 29 =

24 12 124 ÷ 104 =

25 42 × 19 =

26 Subtract the smallest number below from the largest.

10.007   10.077   10.708   10.070   10.780   _____

27 The **mean** of four numbers is $5\frac{1}{2}$. If one of the numbers is 7, what is the **mean** of the other three numbers?

_____

Three numbers multiplied together equal 2880.

A × B × C = 2880   A × B = 360   A × C = 160

28 A =

29 B =

30 C =

The flag is rotated three times about different points and different amounts of a full turn.

Each rotation starts about the position shown.

Draw each new position:

31 Half turn about $(-1, 0)$.

32 Quarter turn clockwise about $(0, 3)$.

33 Quarter turn anticlockwise about $(-2, 0)$.

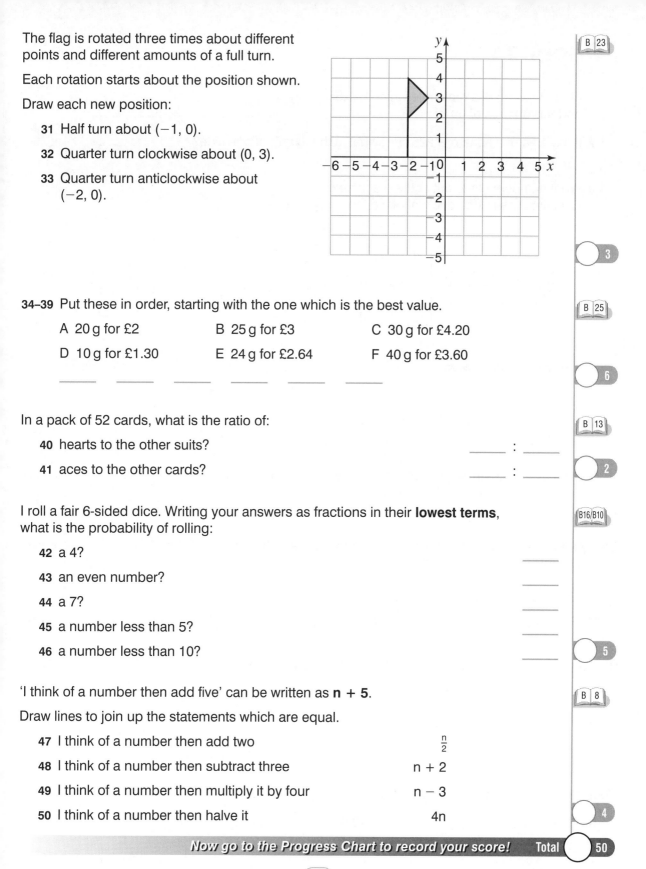

B 23

3

34–39 Put these in order, starting with the one which is the best value.

A 20 g for £2   B 25 g for £3   C 30 g for £4.20

D 10 g for £1.30   E 24 g for £2.64   F 40 g for £3.60

_____   _____   _____   _____   _____   _____

B 25

6

In a pack of 52 cards, what is the ratio of:

40 hearts to the other suits?

41 aces to the other cards?

_____ : _____

_____ : _____

B 13

2

I roll a fair 6-sided dice. Writing your answers as fractions in their **lowest terms**, what is the probability of rolling:

42 a 4?

43 an even number?

44 a 7?

45 a number less than 5?

46 a number less than 10?

B16/B10

5

'I think of a number then add five' can be written as **n + 5**.

Draw lines to join up the statements which are equal.

47 I think of a number then add two $\frac{n}{2}$

48 I think of a number then subtract three $n + 2$

49 I think of a number then multiply it by four $n - 3$

50 I think of a number then halve it $4n$

B 8

4

Now go to the Progress Chart to record your score!   Total   50

Paper 14

1 Find the width of a rectangle which is 7.5 m long, and has an area of 60 m². _____

2 If the area of a square is 225 cm², what is the length of one side? _____

3–6 What numbers come out of the machine?
Give answers to one decimal place where appropriate.

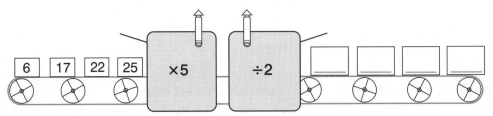

Underline the correct answer.

7 $3^2 =$ 9   27   6   33

8 1.05 m =   150 mm   15 cm   1050 cm   105 cm

9 What is the length of one side of an equilateral triangle if the perimeter of the triangle is 10.5 cm? _____

Give your answers to the following as **mixed numbers**, with fractions in their **lowest terms**.

10 $7\frac{1}{3} - 3\frac{4}{9} =$ _____

11 $3\frac{3}{10} - 1\frac{3}{5} =$ _____

12 $5\frac{2}{8} - 3\frac{11}{16} =$ _____

13 $4\frac{5}{6} - 2\frac{1}{18} =$ _____

Remember to work out brackets first, then ÷ and ×, then + and −.

Find the answers to the following.

14 $5 + 3 \times 2 =$ _____

15 $(12 - 2) \div 5 =$ _____

16 $54 - 4 \times 12 =$ _____

17 $65 + 25 \div 5 =$ _____

Round the following to the nearest **integer**.

18 −31.53 _____

19 12.95 _____

20 29.09 _____

21 −0.41 _____

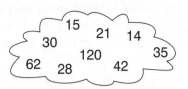

22–25 Write the multiples of 5 from the numbers above.

_____ _____ _____ _____

26–30 Write the multiples of 7 from the numbers above.

_____ _____ _____ _____ _____

31–35 'Multiply by seven then subtract three' can be written as **7n − 3**.

Draw lines to join up the statements which are equal.

Multiply by three then add two $\frac{n}{3} - 2$

Multiply by two then add three $3n + 2$

Divide by two then subtract three $3(n + 2)$

Divide by three then subtract two $2n + 3$

Add two then multiply by three $\frac{n}{2} - 3$

The letters from the word **MATHEMATICS** are placed in a tub and a letter is taken out at random.

Writing your answers as fractions in their **lowest terms**, what is the probability of taking out a letter:

36 S? _____   **37 E?** _____

38 M? _____   **39 T?** _____

Write either **acute**, **obtuse** or **reflex** to describe the angles in the shape below.

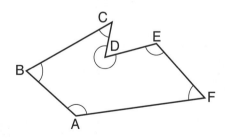

40 ∠ ABC _____   **41** ∠ BCD _____

42 ∠ CDE _____   **43** ∠ DEF _____

44 ∠ EFA _____

Angus, Belinda and Christine had £1.68 between them. After Angus paid back the 3p that he had borrowed from Belinda, and Christine had repaid 5p she had borrowed from Belinda, they found that Angus had twice as much as Belinda, and Belinda had twice as much as Christine.

B4/B13

45–50	At first:	Angus had _____	Belinda had _____	Christine had _____
	Afterwards:	Angus had _____	Belinda had _____	Christine had _____

6

Now go to the Progress Chart to record your score!   Total   50

Paper 15

1–2 Write the next two terms in the following sequence.

B 7

2   3   5   7   11   13   17   19   _____   _____

2

Here are three shaded cubes.

B 21

 A   B   C

Which cubes could have the following nets? (More than one cube may be possible.)

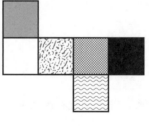

3 _____

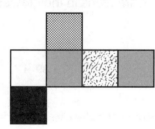

4 _____

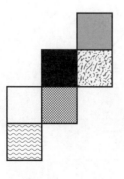

5 _____

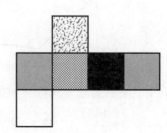

6 _____

4

7–13 All these rectangles have the same perimeter. Find the missing lengths and areas. B 20

Perimeter	Length	Width	Area
24 cm	5 cm	7 cm	35 cm²
24 cm	_____	3 cm	27 cm²
24 cm	1 cm	_____	_____
24 cm	_____	10 cm	_____
24 cm	_____	_____	36 cm²

7

Your task is to guide the robot along the white squares on the plan.
It starts and finishes on the squares marked A, B, C, D or E.
It can only move FORWARD, TURN RIGHT 90° and TURN LEFT 90°.

B 17

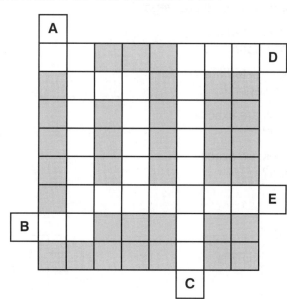

What is the next instruction to get:

14 from C to B via the shortest route?

FORWARD 3, TURN LEFT 90°, _____ , …

15 from A to C with the least number of instructions?

FORWARD 1, TURN LEFT 90°, FORWARD 1, TURN RIGHT 90°, _____ , …

16 from D to B via the longest route without going over any squares more than once?

FORWARD 3, TURN LEFT 90°, FORWARD 5, TURN RIGHT 90°, _____ , …

17 What is the starting instruction to get from E to A with the most number of instructions, (without going over any squares more than once)? _____ , …

4

CHICAGO Illinois									Distances in miles
1020	**DENVER** Colorado								
270	1280	**DETROIT** Michigan							
1650	710	1900	**GRAND CANYON** Ariz.						
1090	1030	1340	1210	**HOUSTON** Texas					
1010	1700	1000	1800	920	**JACKSONVILLE** Flor.				
1770	780	2030	310	1420	2100	**LAS VEGAS** Nevada			
2100	1130	2350	530	1550	2390	280	**LOS ANGELES** Cal.		
1410	2060	1440	2310	1230	360	2520	2730	**MIAMI** Florida	
850	1860	570	2510	1860	1400	2590	2920	1790	**MONTREAL** Quebec
940	1280	1090	1540	360	590	1720	1900	910	1640 **NEW ORLEANS** Louis.

Use the chart to answer these questions.

18 How much further is it from Jacksonville to Miami than from Grand Canyon to Las Vegas? _____

19 Which two places listed are the shortest distance apart? _____ and _____

20 Which two places listed are the greatest distance apart? _____ and _____

21 Which two places are exactly 1700 miles apart? _____ and _____

22 Which two places are exactly 1000 miles apart? _____ and _____

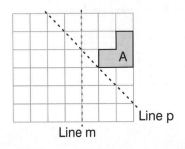
Line p
Line m

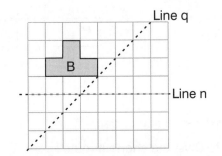
Line q
Line n

23 Reflect shape A in mirror line p. Label it P.

24 Reflect shape A in mirror line m. Label it M.

25 Reflect shape B in mirror line q. Label it Q.

26 Reflect shape B in mirror line n. Label it N.

27 A typist averages 14 words to a line and 30 lines to a page.

How many pages will be needed for 38 406 words? _____

5

4
1

What are the missing numbers?

−8	−5	−2
−11	−8	−5
x	−11	−8

−9	−2	y
−16	−9	−2
−23	−16	−9

z	−51	−105
−51	−105	−159
−105	−159	−213

28 $x =$ _____

29 $y =$ _____

30 $z =$ _____

Car park charges	
Up to 1 hour	£1.00
1 to 2 hours	£1.20
2 to 3 hours	£1.40
3 to 4 hours	£1.60
4 to 5 hours	£1.80
5 to 6 hours	£2.00
6 to 7 hours	£2.20
7 to 8 hours	£2.40
Over 8 and up to 12 hours	£3.00

What would the following people pay?

31 Mrs Ward parked from 8:30 a.m. to 5:05 p.m.   _____

32 Mr Wu parked from 1:05 p.m. to 2:10 p.m.   _____

33 Mrs Bell parked from 2:17 p.m. to 10:01 p.m.   _____

34 Mr Green parked from 10:44 a.m. to 4:05 p.m.   _____

Change these measurements to centimetres.

35 47.5 m _____   **36** 0.176 m _____

37 6.07 m _____   **38** 103.03 m _____

Change these measurements to metres.

39 0.37 km _____   **40** 11 km _____

41 0.002 km _____   **42** 4.15 km _____

Complete the table below.

43–48

Fraction	Decimal	Percentage
$\frac{9}{10}$	_____	_____ %
_____	0.01	_____ %
_____	_____	17%

6

Find the value for x in each of these equations.

B 8

49 $2x + 6 = 14$ $x = $ _____

50 $4x - 3 = 13$ $x = $ _____

2

Now go to the Progress Chart to record your score!   **Total**   50

Paper 16

1–2 Write the next two terms in the following sequence.

B 7

     23   18   11   2   _____   _____

2

Here are some irregular **polygons**. Say whether they are concave or convex and name them.

B 19

Example convex decagon

3–4   _____   _____

5–6   _____   _____

4

Here is part of a train timetable.

B 27

Train	Greasby	Upton	Moreton	Leasowe
A	13:15	13:23	13:29	13:50
B	14:09	14:17	⟶	14:38
C		14:32	14:39	14:59
D	15:01	⟶	15:14	
E		16:07	16:14	16:32

7 What is the shortest travelling time from Greasby to Leasowe?   _____ minutes

8 How many trains will take you from Greasby to Upton? _____

9 If you arrived at Greasby station at 2 p.m. and took the quickest route to Moreton you would arrive at Moreton _____ minutes later.

10 If you arrived at Greasby station at 2.10 p.m. how long would it take you to get to Leasowe? _____

4

What are the missing numbers?

B 7

47.5	34.1	20.7
60.9	47.5	34.1
x	60.9	47.5

159.3	102.5	y
216.1	159.3	102.5
272.9	216.1	159.3

z	32.81	26.03
32.81	26.03	19.25
26.03	19.25	12.47

11 $x =$ _____   **12** $y =$ _____   **13** $z =$ _____

3

I roll a fair 6-sided dice. Writing your answers in their **lowest terms**, what is the probability of rolling:

B16/B10

14 a 6? _____   **15** an odd number? _____

16 a zero? _____   **17** a number greater than 1? _____

18 a number less than 7 and more than 0? _____

5

Indicate which is larger by writing $>$ or $<$ in each space.

A 6
B11/B25

19 0.30 _____ 0.50   **20** 2.6 _____ 2.5

21 5.6 km _____ 5500 m   **22** 0.463 _____ 0.473

4

23–25 Some children from our school went on a day trip to London. The cost was £20.00 per child. Complete the table for the cost per class.

B3/B15
B 12

Class	Number in class	Number going on trip	Cost for the class
2a	30	6	_____
2b	30	7	_____
3a	30	8	_____
3b	30	4	£80
4a	30	13	£260
4b	30	12	£240

26 What is the **range** of the number of pupils from each class? _____

27 Which is the modal class (**mode**)? _____

28 What percentage of 4b are on the trip? _____%

29–34 Now make a bar chart to show how much money was collected from each class.

35 In **lowest terms**, what fraction of all the children from these classes went on this trip?

_____

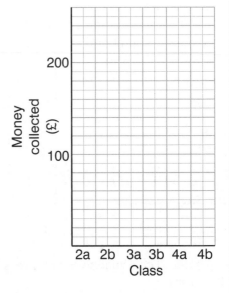

Simplify the following expressions.

36 $6a + a + 3 =$ _____

37 $b + 4b + 4 =$ _____

38 $3c + 4 + 2 =$ _____

39 $5a - 2a + 5 =$ _____

Find the **mode** of the following series.

40 43   44   46   47   43   45   The **mode** is _____

41 101   110   111   100   10   110   The **mode** is _____

42 36   37   33   35   33   39   The **mode** is _____

43 21   31   22   21   32   23   The **mode** is _____

The perimeter of a piece of card is 100 cm and it is four times as long as it is wide.

44 The length is _____ .

45 The width is _____ .

What is the length of the side of a square with an area of:

46 196 cm^2 ? _____

47 289 cm^2 ? _____

What is the order of rotational symmetry of the following shapes?

Square   Regular hexagon

48 order _____   **49** order _____   **50** order _____

Paper 17

1–3 Circle the three **prime numbers**.

16   17   18   19   20   21   22   23

3

Some pupils from Class 5 were asked how long it took them to get to school. Here are their times in minutes.

B 14

| 34 | 42 | 46 | 41 | 32 | 38 | 37 | 24 | 23 | 28 | 27 |
| 32 | 41 | 44 | 43 | 33 | 38 | 36 | 22 | 21 | 26 | 27 |

4–9 Complete this frequency Table A.

Time in minutes	21–25	26–30	31–35	36–40	41–45	46 and over
No. of pupils						

10–12 Now complete this frequency Table B.

Time in minutes	0–20	21–60	61–80
No. of pupils			

13 Which frequency table do you think gives the most useful information about the time it took the pupils to get to school? _____

10

Look at this shape. Work out the area of:

B20/B18

14 the whole shape. _____

15 the shaded part. _____

16 the unshaded part. _____

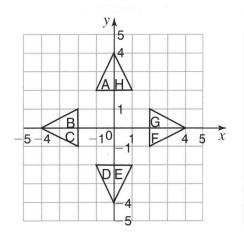

20 cm

8 cm

3

Triangle E is rotated about the origin (0, 0).

B 23

17–19 Which of the triangles A to H are a rotation of E about the origin?

_____   _____   _____

3

47

Underline the correct answer.

20 Days in 2010 =   330   366   160   350   365

21 1% of 1000   =   100   10   1   1000   101

22 3030 m   =   303 km   30.3 km   3.03 km   3.003 km   0.303 km

23 515 cm   =   5.15 m   0.515 m   51.5 m   5150 m   515.5 m

24 40% of 25   =   65   15   12.5   8   10

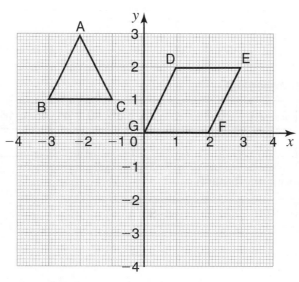

Give the **coordinates** of the letters:

25 D (—— , ——)

26 E (—— , ——)

27 F (—— , ——)

28 G (—— , ——)

Reflect triangle ABC in the x-axis.

Give the **coordinates** of the letters:

29 A′ (—— , ——)   **30** B′ (—— , ——)   **31** C′ (—— , ——)

Rotate **parallelogram** DEFG 90° clockwise about the origin.

Give the **coordinates** of the letters:

32 D′ (—— , ——)

33 E′ (—— , ——)

34 F′ (—— , ——)

35 G′ (—— , ——)

36 How many more lines of symmetry does the triangle have than the **parallelogram**?   _____

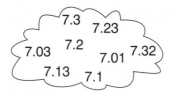

Which two numbers:

37–38 add to give 14.5? _____ _____

39–40 subtract to give 0.27? _____ _____

41–42 add to give 14.55? _____ _____

43–44 subtract to give 0.31? _____ _____

45–46 add to give 14.21? _____ _____

Find the **lowest common multiple** of:

47 3 and 4. _____   **48** 4 and 6. _____

49 2 and 5. _____   **50** 6 and 9. _____

Now go to the Progress Chart to record your score!   **Total** 50

Paper 18

1–3   IN   OUT

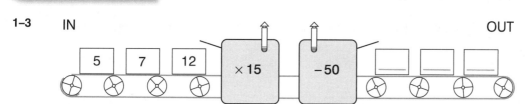

The letters from the word **BANANAS** are placed in a tub and a letter is taken out at random. Writing your answers as fractions in their **lowest terms**, what is the probability of taking out a letter:

4 S? _____   **5 A?** _____

6 N? _____   **7 T?** _____

Indicate which is the larger by writing $>$ or $<$ in each space.

8 24×4 _____ $25 + 60$ **9** $9 + 8 - 4$ _____ $20 - 2 - 6$

10 5×11 _____ 7×8 **11** 9×12 _____ 10×11

12 7×10 _____ 6×12 **13** $3 + 7 + 9$ _____ $2 + 9 + 6$

For each of these shapes, give the area of the whole shape, the area of the shaded part and the area of the unshaded part.

B 20

30 cm

16 cm

10 cm

20 cm

14 Area of whole _____

15 Area of shaded part _____

16 Area of unshaded part _____

20 cm

10 cm

15 cm

5 cm

17 Area of whole _____

18 Area of shaded part _____

19 Area of unshaded part _____

6

A

5 cm

2 cm   4 cm

B

2 cm

2 cm   6 cm

C

7 cm

1 cm   2 cm

D

3 cm

3 cm   3 cm

B 22

20 The volume of Figure A is _____

21 The volume of Figure B is _____

22 The capacity of Figure C is _____

23 The capacity of Figure D is _____

If the sides of each figure were twice as long, what would the volume of each shape be?

24 Figure A _____

25 Figure B _____

26 Figure C _____

27 Figure D _____

8

28–33 Complete the following table.

B 7

3	2	7	___	8	___	21	24
27	18	___	90	___	108	___	___

6

B4/B3

34 Felt-tip pens cost a shopkeeper £1.80 for 7.
How many can he buy with £36.00? _____

35 Carelessly, Lena divided by 8 instead of multiplying
by 9 and got an answer of 564. What should it have been? _____

2

50

What is the **mode** in each series of numbers below?

B 15

36 11	12	14	12	13	15		**Mode** is _____
37 7	9	8	6	9	5		**Mode** is _____
38 24	22	23	21	20	24		**Mode** is _____
39 6	3	3	5	3	4		**Mode** is _____

4

Foreign countries (outside Europe) are listed as Zone 1 or Zone 2 for postal charges (air mail).

B 2

Argentina, Brazil, Canada, Chile and Cuba are in Zone 1.

Tonga, New Zealand, the Philippines, Mongolia, Korea and Japan are in Zone 2.

Up to and including:	Zone 1	Zone 2
100 g	£2.05	£2.33
120 g	£2.40	£2.75
140 g	£2.75	£3.17
160 g	£3.10	£3.59
180 g	£3.45	£4.01
200 g	£3.80	£4.43

How much more does it cost in pence, to send:

40 a 140 g letter to New Zealand than to Canada?   _____

41 a 170 g letter to Korea than to Chile?   _____

42 a 110 g letter to Japan than to Cuba?   _____

43 a 151 g letter to Mongolia than to Chile?   _____

44 a 132 g letter to the Philippines than to Argentina?   _____

5

45 What number, when multiplied by 36, gives the same answer as
42 × 18?   _____

B 3

1

Describe the following **polygons** by name and say whether they are regular or irregular.

B 19

46 [ ]   _____ quadrilateral

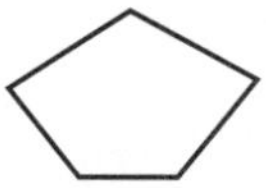

5

Now go to the Progress Chart to record your score!   Total   50

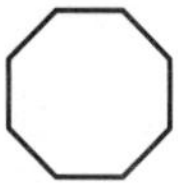

Paper 19

B 6

1 The temperature increases by 6 °C from −2 °C.
What is the new temperature? _____°C

2 The temperature decreases by 13 °C from 4 °C.
What is the new temperature? _____°C

2

Complete the table below.

B 15

3–11

	Mode	Median	Range
$10\frac{1}{2}$ 23 2 $10\frac{1}{2}$	_____	_____	_____
56 221 34 221 −2	_____	_____	_____
33 −3 −65 −3 2	_____	_____	_____

9

Find the **lowest common multiple** of:

B 5

12 3 and 5. _____

13 10 and 15. _____

14 14 and 21. _____

15 3 and 12. _____

4

Prize money to the value of £50 is shared between two friends. Phil gets $\frac{3}{10}$ and
Kusum gets $\frac{7}{10}$.

B 10

16 Phil gets £ _____ .   **17** Kusum gets £ _____ .

2

Here are the shoe sizes of 20 children. First complete the table below and then complete the bar chart.

18–24

2	3	2	1	$1\frac{1}{2}$	$2\frac{1}{2}$	$1\frac{1}{2}$
$1\frac{1}{2}$	$2\frac{1}{2}$	$3\frac{1}{2}$	3	4	$2\frac{1}{2}$	4
3	$3\frac{1}{2}$	3	$2\frac{1}{2}$	4	$2\frac{1}{2}$	

Shoe size	Frequency
1	
$1\frac{1}{2}$	
2	
$2\frac{1}{2}$	
3	
$3\frac{1}{2}$	
4	

7

25–31

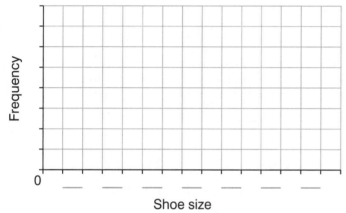

Frequency

0

Shoe size

7

32–34 Complete these shapes. The dashed line is the line of symmetry.

B 24

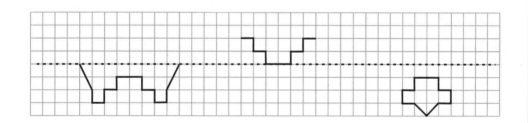

3

A bottle of concentrated orange squash costs 75p and holds 1.25 litres. Each glass holds 300 ml of liquid. 50 ml of orange squash needs to be poured into each glass before adding water.

35 What fraction of the glass would the orange concentrate fill? _____

B 10

36 How many glasses could be made from a bottle of orange squash? _____

B 25

37 If 175 people asked for a drink, how many bottles of orange squash would be needed? _____

B 3

38 How much would it cost to provide 175 people with a drink? _____ B 3

39 If each person was charged 10p for a drink, how much
profit would be made? _____

B3/B2

B 4

5

These scales are used to weigh three parcels. How much does each parcel cost to post?

B14/B26

PARCELS Weight not over:	£
1 kg	5.60
2 kg	6.45
4 kg	8.25
6 kg	9.45
8 kg	10.50
10 kg	13.00

A

B

C

40 A would cost _____   **41** B would cost _____   **42** C would cost _____

43 How much less would it cost to send all three parcels as one large parcel? _____

4

Using a protractor, measure the following angles to the nearest 2°. They are all even numbers (e.g. 12° or 14°).

B 26

44 _____°   **45** _____°   **46** _____°

3

Take two identical cubes and join them together by matching face to face so you cannot see the join.

B 21

For the new object, find the:

47 number of faces. _____

48 number of **vertices**. _____

49 number of **edges**. _____

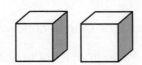

50 How many of the faces of the original cubes can you no longer see? _____

4

Now go to the Progress Chart to record your score!   **Total** 50

Paper 20

B2/B3

If the sum of the digits of a number is divisible by 9, then the number is divisible by 9.

Example 342   3 + 4 + 2 = 9   9 ÷ 9 = 1   so 342 is divisible by 9

1–3 Underline the numbers which are divisible by 9.

3114   57 502   4123   75 501   341 583   3 415 833

3

Here are the petrol gauges of four cars.

B26/B3

 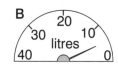  

Petrol costs 70p per litre. To fill up their tanks:

4–5 A would need _____ litres.   This would cost _____ .

6–7 B would need _____ litres.   This would cost _____ .

8–9 C would need _____ litres.   This would cost _____ .

10–11 D would need _____ litres.   This would cost _____ .

8

There are 12 balls in a bag; they are numbered 1 to 12. Writing your answers as fractions in their **lowest terms**, what is the chance of picking:

B16/B10
B 5

12 an odd-numbered ball?   _____

13 a ball which has a multiple of 3 on it?   _____

14 a ball which has a multiple of 5 on it?   _____

15 a ball which has a multiple of 7 on it?   _____

4

Simplify the following expressions.

B 8

16 $15a - 4a + 5 - 3 =$ _____

17 $4b + 9b + 4 + 13 =$ _____

18 $3c + 4 + 5 - 6 - c =$ _____

19 $58p - 32p + 13 + 4 =$ _____

4

Underline the correct answer.

B6/B11
B 10

20 5^2 is   5   25   125

21 2.7 is between   2 and $2\frac{1}{4}$ $2\frac{1}{2}$ and 3 $2\frac{1}{4}$ and $2\frac{1}{2}$

22 $\sqrt{16}$ is   4   8   2

23 $1\frac{1}{1000}$ is   1.1   1.001   1.01

4

Underline the correct answer.

24	Degrees in half a right angle	50	60	90	45	120
25	Minutes in $2\frac{1}{2}$ hours	120	150	140	160	200
26	3^2	5	6	2	9	12
27	Hours in November	600	300	700	800	720
28	Millimetres in 2 metres	1000	100	2000	200	20
29	cm³ in 1 litre	100	10	50	1000	2000

What fraction is shaded in the following circles? Write each fraction in its **lowest terms**.

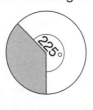
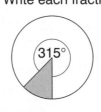

30 _____   **31** _____   **32** _____   **33** _____

What is the total surface area of the following shapes?

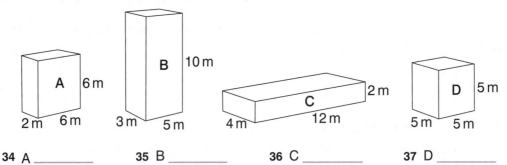

34 A _____   **35** B _____   **36** C _____   **37** D _____

What percentage of each shape is shaded? Write the answer in the space provided.

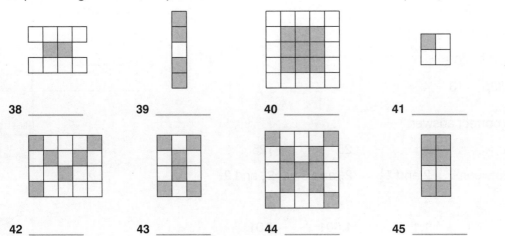

38 _____   **39** _____   **40** _____   **41** _____

42 _____   **43** _____   **44** _____   **45** _____

56

Write the next two terms in the following sequences.

B 7

46–47 1 4 9 16 25 _____ _____

48–49 1 3 6 10 15 _____ _____

4

Sarah spends $\frac{1}{5}$ of the week at work sorting out paperwork. She works 45 hours per week.

B3/B10

50 How many hours of paperwork does Sarah do during two weeks? _____

1

Now go to the Progress Chart to record your score!   Total   50

Paper 21

1

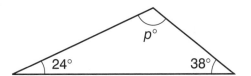

Angle p = _____ °

B 18

1

Using the approximate figures in the conversion table, convert the following measurements from metric to imperial or vice versa.

B 25

2 _____ kilograms ≈ 11 lb

3 2 kilometres ≈ _____ miles

4 _____ litres ≈ $10\frac{1}{2}$ pints

5 15 kilograms ≈ _____ lb

Metric	Imperial
1 litre	$1\frac{3}{4}$ pints
1 kilogram	2.2 lb
8 kilometres	5 miles

4

B 6

6 The temperature is −2 °C. It rises by 5 °C then falls by 8 °C.
What is the new temperature?   _____ °C

7 The temperature is 3 °C. It falls by 9 °C, then rises by 4 °C.
What is the new temperature?   _____ °C

2

Describe the following **polygons** by name and say whether they are regular or irregular.

B 19

8–9

_____ _____

10–11

_____ _____

12–13

_____ _____

6

Work out the following.

14 $\frac{3}{7}$ of €42 = € _____

15 $\frac{4}{7}$ of €4200 = € _____

Translate shape A a shown below. Draw and label each new location.

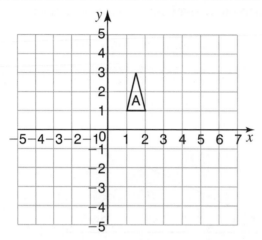

$$b = \begin{pmatrix} 2 \\ 0 \end{pmatrix}$$

$$c = \begin{pmatrix} -3 \\ 0 \end{pmatrix}$$

$$d = \begin{pmatrix} 0 \\ 2 \end{pmatrix}$$

$$e = \begin{pmatrix} -4 \\ 0 \end{pmatrix}$$

$$f = \begin{pmatrix} 4 \\ -4 \end{pmatrix}$$

16 Translate A by **b** to B.　　**17** Translate A by **c** to C.　　**18** Translate A by **d** to D.

19 Translate A by **e** to E.　　**20** Translate A by **f** to F.

What is the volume of these cuboids? They are made from 1-cm cubes.

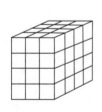 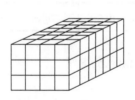 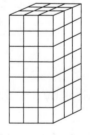 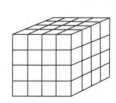

21 _____ cm³　　**22** _____ cm³　　**23** _____ cm³　　**24** _____ cm³

If another layer of 1-cm cubes was placed on top of each cuboid what would the volume be now?

25 _____ cm³　　**26** _____ cm³　　**27** _____ cm³　　**28** _____ cm³

29 Find the difference between six thousand and six and 4567.　　_____

30–34 Place these numbers in order from smallest to largest.

　　−4.1　　2.1　　−3.1　　0.1　　−2.1

_____　_____　_____　_____　_____

Circle the **lowest common multiple** of:

35 8 and 10.	8	10	24	40	80	800
36 24 and 18.	18	24	48	72	180	240
37 15 and 20.	15	20	35	40	60	300

The ages of our family add up to 85 years. I am 10 years old, Dad is $3\frac{1}{2}$ times as old as I am. My sister is 2 years younger than I am and Mum is 4 times as old as my sister.

38 Mum is _____ . **39** Dad is _____ . **40** My sister is _____ .

Remember to work out brackets first, then ÷ and × then + and −.
Find the answers to the following:

41 $(4 + 5) - 5 \div 2$ _____ **42** $22 + 18 \times (9 + 1)$ _____

43 $(19 + 25) \div 4 - 2$ _____ **44** $64 + 26 \div 2$ _____

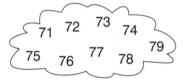

45–46 Write the multiples of 4 from the numbers above. _____ _____

47–49 Write the multiples of 3 from the numbers above. _____ _____ _____

50 Write the multiple of 9 from the numbers above. _____

Now go to the Progress Chart to record your score! **Total** ◯ 50

Paper 22

What is the order of rotational symmetry of each of the following shapes?

1
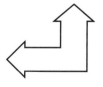

2 Equilateral triangle _____

3

_____

Give the answers to the following in their **lowest terms**.

4 $\frac{7}{8} \times \frac{40}{49} =$ _____

5 $\frac{4}{9} \times \frac{27}{24} =$ _____

6 $\frac{5}{11} \times \frac{66}{50} =$ _____

7 $\frac{4}{5} \times \frac{20}{28} =$ _____

B 10
4

Find the areas of the following right-angled triangles.

B 18

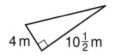

$2\frac{1}{2}$ cm

8 cm

8 Area = _____ cm^2

4.6 cm

2 cm

9 Area = _____ cm^2

4 m $10\frac{1}{2}$ m

10 Area = _____ m^2

6 m

3 m

11 Area = _____ m^2

4

12 Three numbers multiplied together give 2618. One number is 11 and another is 14. What is the third number? _____

B 3
1

The answers to the following questions will be found in this sausage shape.

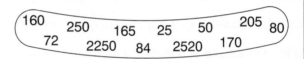

160   250   165   25   50   205   80
72   2250   84   2520   170

B27/B25

13 How many minutes in $2\frac{3}{4}$ hours? _____ minutes

14 How many cm in 2.5 metres? _____ cm

15 How many mm in 2.25 metres? _____ mm

3

16–31 Insert a sign in each space to make each line and column work out to the given answer.

B2/B3

2		3		4	=	10
4		1		2	=	3
2		4		3	=	5
=		=		=		=
8		−1		5	=	2

16

32–36 What are the **prime numbers** more than 25 and less than 45?

B 6

_____   _____   _____   _____   _____

37–41 Draw lines to join up the statements which are equal.

Multiply by four then add three then add two $2n - 3$

Multiply by three then add nine then take two $4n + 5$

Divide by two then multiply by four then subtract three $3(n + 2) - 4$

Divide by three then subtract two then add five $\frac{n}{3} + 3$

Add two then multiply by three then take four $3n + 7$

Answer the following questions only using these words.

Certain   Likely   Unlikely   Impossible

42 A dinosaur will walk down your street tomorrow.   _____

43 I will find some money on the pavement tomorrow.   _____

44 I will roll a six on a single throw with a fair 6-sided dice.   _____

45 I will roll a number higher than two with a fair 6-sided dice.   _____

Here are some nets. Some will make a cuboid and some will not. Write either 'true' if they will or 'false' if they will not.

46 _____   **47** _____   **48** _____

49 _____   **50** _____

Paper 23

1 The temperature is −6 °C. It rises by 15 °C then falls by 20 °C.
What is the new temperature? _____ °C

2 The temperature is 13 °C. It falls by 19 °C then rises by 6 °C.
What is the new temperature? _____ °C

3 The temperature is −13 °C. It falls by 17 °C then rises by 2 °C.
What is the new temperature? _____ °C

Find the surface area of these cuboids.

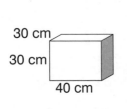

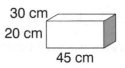

4 _____ cm²   **5** _____ cm²   **6** _____ cm²

Translate shape A as shown below. Draw and label each new location.

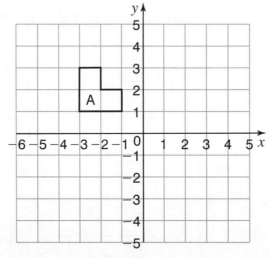

$\mathbf{b} = \begin{pmatrix} 5 \\ 2 \end{pmatrix}$ $\mathbf{c} = \begin{pmatrix} 4 \\ -2 \end{pmatrix}$ $\mathbf{d} = \begin{pmatrix} -1 \\ -4 \end{pmatrix}$ $\mathbf{e} = \begin{pmatrix} -2 \\ 2 \end{pmatrix}$ $\mathbf{f} = \begin{pmatrix} 2 \\ -5 \end{pmatrix}$

7 Translate A by **b** to B.   **8** Translate A by **c** to C.

9 Translate A by **d** to D.   **10** Translate A by **e** to E.

11 Translate A by **f** to F.

Write the number which has a:

12 7 in the tenths place. _____

13 5 in the tens place. _____

14 2 in the units place. _____

15 6 in the thousandths place. _____

16 1 in the hundreds place. _____

17 8 in the hundredths place. _____

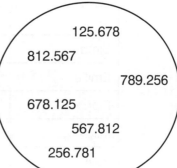

125.678

812.567

789.256

678.125

567.812

256.781

6

Using the approximate figures in the conversion table, convert the following measurements from metric to imperial or vice versa.

18 42 litres ≈ _____ pints

19 1000 kilograms ≈ _____ lb

20 72 kilometres ≈ _____ miles

21 _____ kilometres ≈ $27\frac{1}{2}$ miles

22 _____ litres ≈ 16 pints

Metric	Imperial
1 litre	$1\frac{3}{4}$ pints
1 kilogram	2.2 lb
8 kilometres	5 miles

5

23 What number, when multiplied by 45, will give the same answer as 65 × 27? _____

If £1 is €1.30, indicate which is larger by writing > or < in each space.

24 €0.60 _____ 50p

25 €4.50 _____ £3.50

26 £2.45 _____ €2.54

27 £2.40 _____ €3.15

Complete the table below.

28–36

	Mode	Median	Range
100 300 99 10 000 45	_____	_____	_____
−4 −7 −11 −7	_____	_____	_____
$\frac{1}{2}$ $\frac{3}{4}$ $\frac{1}{2}$ $\frac{3}{4}$ $\frac{1}{2}$ $\frac{3}{4}$ $\frac{1}{2}$	_____	_____	_____

Here are the ages of six friends.

	Years	Months
Simon	11	6
Emilie	10	11
Pippa	11	1
Milo	10	10
Ravi	11	11
Matthew	11	3

37 Their ages add up to: _____

38 Their average age is: _____

39 Another girl joins them and their average age is now
11 years 2 months. How old is the newcomer? _____   **3**

Find the common **factors** of: **B 5**

40–41 15 and 18.   _____ _____

42–45 24 and 32.   _____ _____ _____ _____   **6**

46–50 Complete the table of values to satisfy the rule: $y = 2x + 8$.   **B 8**

x	−2	−1	0	1	2	3
$y = 2x + 8$	____	____	____	____	12	____

12

Now go to the Progress Chart to record your score!   **Total**   **50**

Paper 24

Find the areas of the following right-angled triangles.   **B 18**

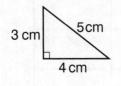

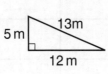

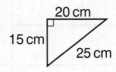

1 _____ cm²   **2** _____ m²   **3** _____ cm²   **4** _____ m²   **4**

64

5	805	6	904	7	590	8	860
	× 407		× 760		× 609		× 570

9–12 Draw four <u>different</u> nets of a closed cube (six square faces) on the grid below. None of your answers should be reflections or rotations of one another.

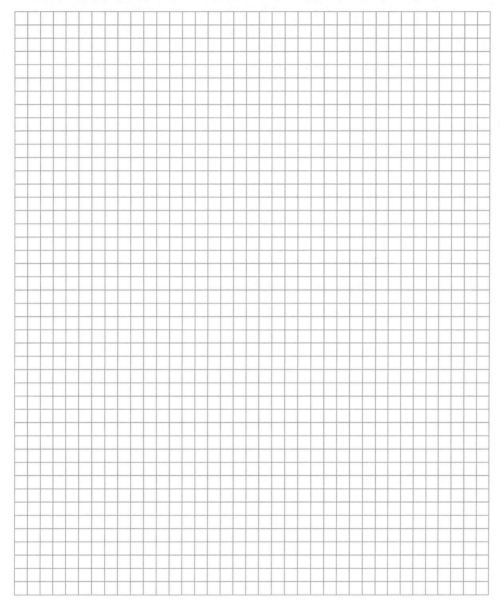

Three sums of money total £100. The largest amount is £46.80, the second largest is three times as large as the smallest.

13 The second largest amount is £ _____

14 The smallest amount is £ _____

Answer the following. Use **mixed numbers** where appropriate and write fractions in their **lowest terms**.

B 10

15 $1\frac{1}{2} \div 1\frac{3}{4} =$ _____

16 $1\frac{3}{4} \div 3\frac{1}{2} =$ _____

17 $2\frac{1}{4} \div 1\frac{1}{2} =$ _____

18 $3\frac{2}{3} \div 1\frac{5}{6} =$ _____

4

Find the highest common **factor** of the following pairs:

B 5

19 40 and 65 _____

20 14 and 35 _____

21 30 and 48 _____

22 10 and 120 _____

23 26 and 30 _____

24 20 and 44 _____

25 36 and 63 _____

7

264 children go home from school by train. One third of them get off at the first station and $\frac{5}{8}$ of these children are girls.

B10/B3
B 2

26 How many girls leave the train at the first station? _____

27 How many boys leave the train at the first station? _____

28 How many children get off after the first station? _____

3

In a village the population is 1010. The men and women together number 451 and the women and children together number 795.

B 2

29–31 There are: _____ men, and _____ women, and _____ children.

3

32 I have £9.00. How many magazines, each costing 59p, can I buy? _____

B 3

1

33–35 If the last two digits of a number are divisible by 4 then the number is divisible by 4.

B2/B3

Example 3424   24 ÷ 4 = 6   so 3424 is divisible by 4.

Underline the numbers which are divisible by 4.

3114   57 532   4123   75 503   341 588   3 415 820

3

Write < or > in each space below.

A 6

36 11^2 _____ 110

B 6

37 35 minutes _____ $\frac{2}{3}$ hours

B 27

2

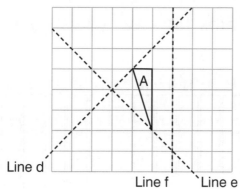

Line d   Line f   Line e

B 23

38 Reflect shape A in mirror line d. Label it D.

39 Reflect shape A in mirror line e. Label it E.

40 Reflect shape A in mirror line f. Label it F.

3

All these rectangles have the same perimeter. Find the missing lengths and the areas.

B 20

41–48

Length	Width	Area
10 cm	8 cm	80 cm²
_____	3 cm	_____
1 cm	_____	_____
_____	2.5 cm	_____
_____	_____	81 cm²

8

B 17

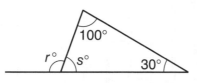

49 Angle *r* = _____ °　　　　　**50** Angle *s* = _____ °

2

Now go to the Progress Chart to record your score!   Total   50

Progress Chart   Maths 11⁺ - 12⁺ years Book 1

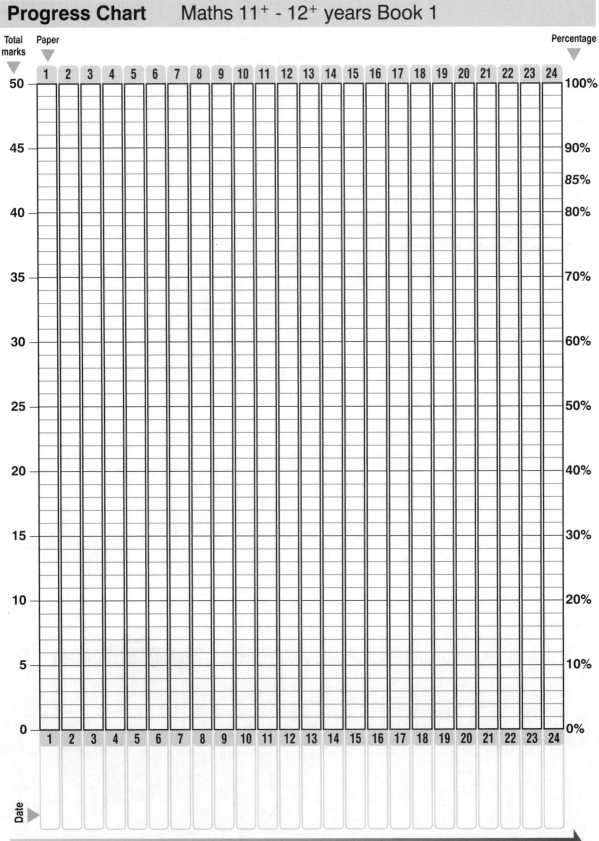

Total marks

Paper

Percentage

When you've finished the book use the Next Steps Planner